Living
at the Edge of
Faith

W9-CFJ-606

Living at the Edge of Faith

Lawrence D. Reimer

Judson Press® Valley Forge

LIVING AT THE EDGE OF FAITH

Copyright © 1984
Judson Press, Valley Forge, PA 19482-0851
Second Printing 1987

All rights reserved. No part of this publication may be reproduced, stored in a retrieval system, or transmitted in any form or by any means, electronic, mechanical, photocopying, recording, or otherwise, without the prior permission of the copyright owner, except for brief quotations included in a review of the book.

The Scripture quotations in this publication are from the Revised Standard Version of the Bible copyrighted 1946, 1952 © 1971, 1973 by the Division of Christian Education of the National Council of the Churches of Christ in the U.S.A., and used by permission.

Library of Congress Cataloging in Publication Data

Reimer, Lawrence D.
  Living at the edge of faith.

  Includes bibliographical references.
  1. Christian life—United Church of Christ authors.
I. Title.
BV4501.2.R436 1984   230′.5834   83-22244
ISBN 0-8170-1023-8

The name JUDSON PRESS is registered as a trademark in the U.S. Patent Office.
Printed in the U.S.A. ⊕

To my wife, Sandy

Acknowledgments

There is an old joke which goes, "I would like to thank the following people, without whom this book would have been written in half the time." All who have supported this effort have also shared their critical tools freely. I could not have done it without them, but what they taught me sure took some time.

I am deeply grateful to the people of the United Church of Gainesville, Florida, who started me and then saw me through this project. They are people who value books and who understood what it meant for me to write. The men's lunch group of the church showed me how to write a proposal and submit it for publication. In particular, Sanford Berg, Leonard Beeghley, and Shannon McCune stayed with me in the process. Judson Press, and my editor, Phyllis Frantz, showed me how to put my ideas into a form suitable for publication. I thank all these people for their faith in this work.

Sandy Reimer, my wife and co-worker in ministry, has the special gift of discerning which of my ideas might go somewhere and which are of no interest to anyone but me. She shares that gift with a unique combination of honesty and care. To her go my deepest thanks.

Contents

Introduction

This is a book for and about people on the edge. These are people who have moved out of the comfortable center of culture and faith, yet who will not leave their roots behind. These are people who find it painful that they are unable to cope with today's issues through the practices and structures of their childhood churches, yet they still yearn for a sense of community not easily found outside the church. These are people who reject the mass movement of this country toward self-assured comforts of moral certainty, yet who want a religious context in which to search out the ethical questions of abortion, war and peace, capital punishment, free speech, and sexual responsibility.

These are people who feel that many of the social programs they fought so hard to establish are now ineffective strategies for carrying out their deepest commitments to justice and equality. Yet they have not discovered new alliances and they are uneasy with new visions. These people seek the healing of spiritual nurture yet resist anything that sounds like a retreat from social concern. These are people who cannot swallow the traditional language of the church any longer, so they struggle for an inclusive way of speaking which does not yet fully exist.

People on the edge are those who have experienced the power of personal responsibility in encounter groups, transactional analysis, Gestalt therapy and the like, yet who are somehow uneasy with just "taking responsibility for myself." They seek a God both in and beyond the here and now. These are people who have explored the gifts of Eastern religions, yet they affirm their Judeo-Christian tradition. They want a community of faith which includes their religious heritage yet also calls them to grow by seeking new dimensions of truth.

People on the edge are those who seek to recognize their brokenness in the shared pain of humankind without being destroyed by it, and accept their holiness in their oneness with God without being deluded by it. They are people who have tasted death in the dying of those close to them and have experienced their own dark night of the soul, yet at the end of their human resources they have been touched by an acceptance which may well be called grace. They are on the edge, living in tension between the old images which are passing away and the new images seeking to be born.

This book is a series of thoughts and conversations arising from a community of people at the edge. The edge is where I place myself, uneasy with the classic confessions of my own Christian tradition yet unwilling to give up this tradition as the path of my spiritual journey. I am a pastor of the United Church of Christ in Gainesville, Florida, and campus minister at the University of Florida. The community which I serve has raised the questions addressed here. I share them because I believe that questions and stories which are authentic in a particular way touch that which is universal in the bond of faith.

While I write from my Protestant Christian experience, the thoughts here have been shaped in interaction with people living out their journeys in Judaism, Roman Catholicism, Eastern religions, and ethical humanism. I believe that all of us on the edge need networks of community in which to express our questions, affirmations, and commitments. Such communities exist throughout this country, but they are often unaware of each other. While their voices are often raised effectively in political and social concern, they are protectively private in matters of faith. It is time to share.

I share with the conviction that there is an element of Christianity which always functions best as a minority opinion. The purpose of the gospel said Paul Scherer, a famous preacher and author, "is not only to comfort the distressed, but to distress the comfortable."[1] Those are saving words for me when my faith sends me to the edge. They underlie what is written here.

---

[1] Paul Scherer, *Love Is a Spendthrift* (New York: Harper & Row, Publishers, Inc., 1961) p. 44.

1

What Is a Realistic Vision of the Spiritual Journey?

Life at its best is a spiritual journey, and religious commitment is a lifelong saga. Yet we live in a goal-oriented society which wants instant certainty and specific destinations. Bumper stickers such as "I Found It!" or "God Said It—I Believe It—That Settles It" suggest a rather belligerent defense of a religious faith which means to get somewhere and then refuses to budge. For those of us on the edge of traditional religious dogma, however, such suggestions of rather premature arrival at eternal answers do not open life to the future.

I have a vision of the spiritual life as a journey whose end is strangely elusive. That vision is related to jogging. Before I go any farther, I want to state that I do not in any way identify with those who experience God at the tenth kilometer of a fifteen kilometer run. I live in a town where running is an epidemic. There are probably more jogging shoes per capita here than television sets. I find endless talk of running to be boring. I do not agree with a recent writer who said that since so many running events are held on Sunday mornings, running must therefore be a religious experience.

With that disclaimer out of the way, I am going to say some good things about jogging. I do jog every other day, about as often as I pray, which is enough to keep me in shape but not so much as to make me into a fanatic. I believe that jogging can be an important part of an integrated life if you are physically able to do it. I fear that too many people make an idol of jogging, using it as a compulsive hedge against death. As I draw some parallels between jogging and the spiritual journey, therefore, remember the pitfalls of worshiping the golden jogging shoe.

Every now and then an eternal truth breaks through clichés, and we greet it with the "aaahh" that is a welcome of God's grace. The advertising firm for Nike running shoes has touched one of these truths. It is summed up in a poster which bears the words "There is no finish line." The poster is a picture of a man running alone along a country highway. The road stretches for miles, and this sense of an eternal path is accentuated by a string of telephone wires stretching out along the side of this road. The road is one of gentle hills surrounded by wild flowers. Under the picture are the words "There is no finish line."

These words apply to any endeavor, but for the moment the truth that there is no finish line is a message already familiar to anyone who jogs. Such is the nature of truth. When you first hear it, it is as if you've known it all your life but had never put it into words until this moment. Suddenly, in this poster, you can see that true commitment takes you beyond prizes, goals, and finish lines to a place where the experience itself carries meaning.

In running there comes a point where your body is comfortable with pushing itself, where your mind is in tune with the rhythm of your steps. You feel your breathing as power rather than weakness. There is an exhilaration in knowing that your blood is flowing freely, that your muscles are gaining strength, and that for the moment your life is integrated into a single purpose. You feel in that moment as if you could run forever. There is no finish line.

To get to this place means deciding one day to put one foot in front of the other enough times to get moving. It means spending a lot of time feeling pain and a certain amount of time feeling foolish. And in the beginning you may wonder rather regularly why you are doing this to yourself.

In the beginning all you do is ask questions. You have to live with the questions in order to get into shape. You have to discipline yourself until the new experience becomes part of your life. You live the question of why.

The spiritual journey is like this. You begin out of a desire to develop a strength that you once may have felt naturally but which now is lost. You begin not because you must but because you want to. You want a dimension in your life that is presently not there. You begin hesitantly, feeling uncomfortable and foolish. In that beginning you ask constantly, "Do I have it right? Is this how it's to be done? Is this what I'm supposed to feel?" No one really has satisfactory answers. If you are too impatient for answers, you quit. If you listen to the advice of too many other people, you find yourself feeling clumsier and clumsier. Finally you simply must decide to spend time exploring the questions of faith in your life even in this confused, beginning time.

Then a transition occurs. You begin to feel the time spent in searching become integrated with the rest of your life. You know that your mind is beginning to function with your heart and soul. The questions themselves become signs of meaning rather than emptiness. You have not arrived at the end of your search; instead you feel the flow, as if you could travel forever, and you understand that this is the point: to live the questions, to travel forever. There is no finish line. The journey was there before your birth and it will continue beyond this life itself. In the journey there will be lapses, different stages, renewed feelings of pain, plateaus, and walls. But there is no finish line and you do not need one. You have accepted your journey as meaningful even though the questions continue.

To be on the edge is to ache for a stronger spiritual foundation. Without such a foundation, little else matters, for it can all pass away. The following two elements of the spiritual journey make the most sense in uncovering that foundation. First is the realization that there is no finish line. Second is the understanding that to experience the meaning of a journey without a finish line requires a commitment to begin in times of uncertainty and questions.

Often it is our very desire to know exactly what this spiritual journey means that blocks us from experiencing it. To be on the edge is to realize that faith is not something we possess; it is a process we live. It is sometimes difficult to accept this because so many have promised answers. They have told us that if we would just let Jesus come into our hearts and get all the Scripture lessons right, we would then have the ultimate experience of faith, find the finish line, and be saved.

I do not see this finality for life at the edge. I see living the

questions, journeying forever without a finish line, and understanding that this is what eternity means—a journey without beginning
or end. There are some pictures of what this journey of faith might
look like, not answers but signposts. Frederick Buechner suggests
that one such picture might be friendship.[1] If you find yourself
asking for proof of a friendship, that relationship is probably already
on the skids. Faith, as the writer of Hebrews (11:1) says, is the
assurance of things hoped for and the conviction of things unseen.
As in a relationship with a friend, faith in God is never proved.
There is no way to prove that your friend is not using you for
selfish ends, but there are moments with your friend when a glance
is caught, laughter is spontaneous, silence is comfortable, that mean
friendship without proof. Friendship is a quality which lives in a
different dimension of required proof. There is no finish line in the
life of friends. There is no goal. Friendship is a process.

Faith in God is like that. It is certainly worthwhile and acceptable
to use your mind to think about God, but nothing worthwhile
about God can ever objectively be guaranteed. Rather it is by
participating in a relationship, experiencing conversations and silence, joy and sorrow with God that an awareness of faith develops
which is unique. There are clear and objective proofs that two plus
two equals four or that two parts hydrogen and one part oxygen
make water, but as Buechner says, you cannot prove that life is
better than death, that beauty is beautiful, or even that you have
free will. Without proof we look for pictures of that which is
unseen, and we find acts of great courage, moments of deep love,
and discoveries of new truth which spring from a core of created
goodness which flows through life like an eternal stream. To believe
in that core even though you cannot prove it, is faith.

A second element of the journey is that faith is on again, off
again rather than once and for all. Paul Tillich said that doubt was
not the opposite of faith but an element of it. This too flies in the
face of our need to achieve. We often want faith as we want a
degree, appointment, or publication. When we want a lifetime
guarantee, we're suckers for the hucksters.

[1] Frederick Buechner, *Wishing Thinking* (Harper & Row, Publishers, Inc., 1973),
p. 26.

The difference between the spiritual journey of the Christian faith and the novocaine for the mind that passes for faith in so many smile-oriented crusades, Christian and otherwise, that I encounter on campus is that Christian faith is on again, off again. The groups which we call cults for lack of a better label, promise an endless weekend, a constant religious high that never goes away. This is not the race we run. There is meaning in the Christian tradition of the week. There is a routine of a sabbath on Sunday, work during the week, recreation on weekends, including that sabbath renewal of community worship. Sometimes we criticize this routine as superficial, but look at it again. Faith is a cycle of highs and lows, ebb and flow, creating and receiving, speaking and hearing, protesting and praying. One University of Florida professor of religion calls those who seek after nothing but the mountaintop experience, "bliss ninnies."

How then do we get on this up-and-down path of the spiritual journey? Here the running analogy is the strongest. The key is the willingness to be open to a relationship with God and to keep striving for this openness daily, weekly, monthly. It is difficult to begin a path leading to a destiny which is so unclear without intentionally being open. It is easy to stop growing spiritually just as it is easy to get lazy physically, becoming stiff and grouchy when we do not open ourselves to seek a greater strength.

I have long respected the commitment necessary to stick with social causes. In fact I have done well in sticking with my own favorite social issues. I stay involved in the usual liberal arena— peace movements, prisons, community agencies, and the schools. I do not intend to substitute personal piety for that kind of involvement. But now I see how important it is to search the paths of spiritual healing and follow them with the same discipline I apply to these social concerns. Meditation, prayer, daily devotion, yoga, journal writing, a psalm, and silence—these are avenues of spiritual journeying and one must make a choice to follow them and a commitment to stay with them to find a center for an open life.

The jogging parallels ultimately fade away, for none of us can keep our body running forever. "That which we can see," says Paul, "passes away. But that which cannot be seen lasts forever" (paraphrase of 2 Corinthians 4:18b). The journey of faith looks beyond visible finish lines, with assurance of things unseen, conviction of things hoped for. It trusts that in the journeying is the silent enfolding eternity of God.

There is a stride we can reach in the spiritual journey where traveling feels much like the pace of the runner in the Nike poster who has passed the barrier of wanting finish lines, rewards, and answers. This stride no longer seeks a reserved seat in heaven, approval from religious leaders, or a promise of a mind without worries. We discover here that the journey is eternal and that is enough.

Questions for Reflection

1. What experiences in your life, jogging and otherwise, have taken you to a place where there are no finish lines (e.g., music, writing, painting, dancing, parenting, hiking, etc.)?

2. If you were writing a book on your spiritual journey, what would be the title of the present chapter in your life?

3. If faith involves "living the questions," what questions are you living right now?

4. Draw a time line of your life which depicts the "hills and valleys" of faith in your life. Do you see a pattern? What does this time line tell you about where you are now?

5. Do you keep a sabbath time for rest and renewal? What is it, and what does it mean to you?

2

What Do We Do with
Our Embarrassment of Riches?

The spiritual journey then is one which has no finish line. "Live the questions," says the poet Rilke,[1] which is the best advice one can give for life at the edge, for the probing search of faith doesn't necessarily solve the dilemmas of life.

But that is not the whole picture. Remember, within the journey itself are times of ebb and flow. Life flows even at the edge, and in those moments we do experience great riches. Chapter one focused largely on the struggle of the journey. In this chapter we see that adult faith is a time of both powerful pain and embarrassing riches. Both are inevitable. We must deal with both.

Let's get pain out of the way first. I have a hunch that we are better at coping with pain than riches. We do better at discovering faith in times of difficulty than in times of success. Those who have gone through a recent crisis can tell the most about prayer, grace, and the strong hand of God which pulled them through. My own devotional journal has the most entries in the times when I have been the most depressed.

Dead ends, hopeless causes, an injured or sick child, life-threatening illness, the loss of a parent, friend, or loved one—these are the pains of adulthood. These are the moments when we have gasped the name of God before we even knew that we had planned to pray. This is appropriate, true, and meaningful. Our faith is refined in the furnace of struggle. My predominant memory of my

[1] Rainer Maria Rilke, *Letters to a Young Poet,* trans. M. D. Herter Norton (New York: W. W. Norton & Co., Inc., 1934).

own teenage faith is that of a deep ache. Coming into my own belief was a struggle, probably because coming into my own life was a struggle. Everything about the future was unknown and the present was shaky. It was a struggle to figure out what I would look like when my body caught up to my feet. I think I went from a size six shoe to a size ten in about one year when I was still five feet tall. In fact, my parents became so accustomed to buying shoes two sizes too big for me that I was graduating from college before I realized that my feet had stopped growing at size ten and I did not need to be walking around in size twelve.

As I struggled to understand how my feet and body would work out, I struggled to understand what love was, or who, if anybody, would love me. It was just as hard to find a faith that was my own and not fed to me by someone else. In fact, at that time faith and struggle were just about synonymous to me.

Faith, however, was born, especially in rebellion against every kind of injustice. I particularly remember the long struggle I went through attending church. I hated irrelevant prayers, the ridiculous words of many hymns, and the pompous nature of the sermons. I just about gave myself teenage ulcers swallowing so much anger in worship. But the anger made me grow. It made me search for clearer words and richer songs. I vowed to preach what mattered in language that could be understood.

Then a strange thing happened. I grew up. I am now the preacher and I preach what I want, select hymns that have meaning, and offer prayers in real language on concerns that matter. I have found a church which is a place of considerable pleasure. And what is good and comfortable is embarrassing. I don't always know how to find faith in the comfortable. I think I have to learn something here.

The situation I am in reminds me of a story of my friend Ben, whom I knew as a student at Yale Divinity School. Ben was a ranting, raving Southern Baptist from Macon, Georgia. His outrage at the injustice of segregation in the church and the world impelled him to ministry and to Yale. His entire commitment in ministry was to right the wrongs of racial injustice. In the midst of one of his speeches, as he called down curses upon the church for its irrelevance, injustice and insensitivity, another student sitting in on this particular discussion interrupted, saying, "Ben, what are you going to do when the race problem is solved?" Ben stopped, fist still raised in the air from his last gesticulation, looked over his shoulder and gasped, "Then . . . I'll preach the gospel."

I think Ben figured he was safe; he'd never have to preach the gospel. We are often like Ben. We count on injustice and pain to fire up our faith, and we don't know what we would do if injustice were righted.

Now I have something very difficult to say. Problems do get solved and when they do, we have to celebrate the gospel as well as preach it. Don't get me wrong. Wars continue. Racism abounds. Sin is always there and death never takes a holiday. But in the midst of this pain, growing up means experiencing the reality that peace sometimes breaks out, races join hands, wounds heal, and even death is robbed of its victory.

A child screams as if a five-minute feeding delay means the end of the world. A teenager sees a lost point, a missed party, a college rejection as the end of all hope for life or love or a career. As adults, each of us has lived through something we once said we would:

    a. never do
    b. never survive
    c. or both.

To grow up is to understand that no matter which turn the road of life takes, it goes on. On the other side of the valley, beyond the pit of despair, there are moments of embarrassing riches. We may have trouble growing in faith from these moments. We have learned how to handle pain. Comfort is embarrassing.

I once knew of a group of former alcoholics that did so well, no one was drinking. This made the group a little nervous, for members had not yet discovered what their function should be once they had succeeded in their initial goal. They needed a drinker, and so a member of the group obliged and started drinking again so the group could fulfill its mission. This cycle continued until the group realized what it was doing and learned how to celebrate its own embarrassment of riches.

We, too, sometimes recycle our own pain when we do not know how to celebrate the good gifts of life. It happens in families, in the church, even in our jobs, in subconscious and unknown ways. Trouble is a familiar feeling, one linked with growth, and we sometimes forget how to live without it.

Like my friend Ben, like the group of former alcoholics, we need to face the moments when we experience an embarrassment of riches. We are rich. By the world's standards we are all rich in goods. We are rich in faith, for we have all come back from the edge from time to time and experienced the good moments of rest and peace. It is important to recognize how to grow from this embarrassing richness so we do not unknowingly sabotage it because its beauty is too gentle. Second, it is important not to take for granted moments of joy, people whom we love and who love us, and the God who sends the sunshine and the rain. If we take them for granted, we may unknowingly give them up and they are not easily found again.

There are times for joy on the journey, times to thank God for the goodness of life as deeply as we pray for release from its pain. More of the Bible speaks from the condition of pain, the moments of repentance and newfound faith, than from comfort. This is especially true of the Gospels and the letters of Paul. But the Psalms, prophets and stories of Israel's history uncover the riches of adult faith in their fullness.

King David suffered the death of a son, the pain of a selfish sexual affair and its destructive consequences, and the arrogance of power. But he also experienced the power of promises kept and the beauty of new songs sung. At the end of his life he found grace in the covenant God made with him that the promise David and God shared together would not be broken for all the generations of humankind to follow. David celebrated the embarrassment of his riches in that covenant.

There are moments when the cup of life runs over in its fullness. Old wounds are healed. The restless groaning of creation ceases. There is a glimpse of peace.

Even for those of us who find our faith at the edge, identifying perhaps more often with pain than promise, these moments come. The struggle is my favorite theme, but the richness of graceful rest is a counterpoint to that theme which always plays beside it.

There is a passage from Scripture which resonates with this richness. It is from Isaiah 40:31.

> They who wait for the LORD shall renew their strength.
> They shall mount up with wings like eagles,
> They shall run and not be weary,
> They shall walk and not faint.

To have grown up in a faith which includes these words is an embarrassment of riches. For we have had our strength renewed more than once. We have known times when we could just barely walk along, but did not faint; times when we ran and did not grow weary. And then there were moments when through some indescribable grace we have mounted up and soared with wings like eagles. Of course we return quickly to the ground. But such running and soaring are glimpses we know of an eternal flight. This is our embarrassment of riches.

Questions for Reflection

1. Do you have as much trouble identifying experiences of faith in times of "embarrassing riches" as in moments of pain and struggle?

2. Consider the images of Isaiah 40.

   a. When have you experienced faith in moments when you could just barely walk along?

   b. When have you found faith in times when you ran but did not grow weary?

   c. When have you found faith in times when you soared like an eagle?

3. How do you celebrate the "embarrassment of riches" in times of rest and peace on the journey of faith?

4. It has been said that the purpose of the gospel is not only to comfort the distressed, but to distress the comfortable. Which side of the equation is most reflective of your experience with the gospel? How might you balance that equation to be equally open to the other side as well?

3

What Do We Do
When Dreams Fail?

I have drawn a picture of life at the edge in which the spiritual journey is one without a finish line, and in that journey we experience both the struggle of living the questions and the embarrassment of restful riches. Part of the meaning of that edge is the precarious way we balance between the comfort of level ground on one side and the uncertainty of the cliff on the other. The next question for and from those who live faith at this edge is, What do we do when our dreams fail? A friend asked me this question and she was referring to dreams in a number of levels. First, what of the obvious dreams—careers, homes, hopes not working out quite the way we had pictured them? She also asked of deeper dreams, How do we face the limitations of our lives? And finally she asked of the deepest dreams, How do we cope with the threat to life itself?

There are two great dangers in responding to these questions from the edge. Either we tilt toward the comfortable ground of the past and respond that the loss of the dream and its subsequent suffering is "God's will," or we lean toward the cliff and mouth an equally inadequate "Live the questions." Each of these phrases has its place and meaning but each has also become a cliché. Adlai Stevenson once said that a cliché is a statement which was true perhaps the first 500 times it was used, then its meaning begins to fall apart. There is truth both in God's will and in the living of the questions, but in limited doses. The structure I will present for dealing with failed dreams may allow these phrases to slip out, but only for a moment.

The problem with most attempts to deal with suffering is that they try to find one response for all levels of pain, evil, and struggle. The result is that the response is either too heavy for minor problems or too light for the major ones. The question of the failure of dreams was posed to me at three levels and at about the same time I heard that three-leveled question, I read of Herbert Butterfield's theory of history which suggests that we live at three levels: free will, natural law, and providence.[1] These three levels run concurrently throughout life and I think they can give us a framework for dealing with the failure of dreams.

At level one is the "American Dream" and free will. Picture your version of the American dream, your dream house, your dream family, your dream life. This level begins with free will. In the beginning we are free to dream as we wish, but dreams of success soon overtake us and build their own structures of happiness. The proper response to the loss of the dream at level one is the restoration of the freedom which began the dream.

There is a good biblical story for this level, but again I caution that this is not a story purporting the loss of deeper dreams. The story I am referring to is one which Jesus tells (Luke 12) of a man who stored his riches in barns thinking he could then sit back and enjoy himself. But in the obsession of building big and secure barns for his wealth, he loses the core of life itself. What of his soul? Where are his riches truly invested? If his lifework is stored in barns where thieves, moths, and rust can destroy, will his heart truly be anywhere else?

The classic American dream is not terribly different from the dream of the barn builder. Even if we do achieve the dream, we wind up like that barn builder, storing up our acquisitions but losing the essence of life itself. Success is an illusion.

The most common experience of the American dream is losing it. The second most common experience is thinking you are the only person who has lost it. Everyone else, it seems, is living the American dream, and you feel like the American failure. But the

[1]Herbert Butterfield, *Christianity and History* (London: G. Bell & Sons, Ltd., 1950).

reality of the human community is that every one of us has lost a dream, which in its ironic way binds us together.

The losses of the American dream are not earthshaking. Level one dream failures are discoveries that happiness cannot be bought, the dream house has a leaky roof, and the sweet taste of success causes cavities. We can continue to let the dream drive us, building more barns, gathering more wealth, like the person in the Bible story, or we can look at another direction for meaning, one which accepts the common experience of brokenness not as failure but as meaning.

To live meaningfully in level one is to live in freedom. We are the dreamers. Every character, every structure in the dreams has our very own name on it. The paradox is that in losing the dream, we experience the freedom of this sphere of life more fully. The loss is real. The shock is not to be denied. But if we recognize that the dream is a myth, then we can see that in its loss we gain our freedom. The American dream is that more will make us happy. The reality is that in this time of inflation, we can beat the spiral of the rising cost of everything only by wanting less. In a time when the national American dream of constantly rising power and success seems to crumble, the good news is that God is not mocked. We reap what we sow and we pay for our luxurious living. Our material standard of living is still higher than that of any nation in the world. The loss of our riches can only serve to bring us closer to our sisters and brothers here and around the world.

Losing the dream is not failure. Failure is succeeding in the dream, gathering all the wealth possible, storing it in barns, and then finding that tonight our soul is required and no wealth is there.

In level one we have the greatest freedom to affect the destiny of our lives.

Now move to level two, where Butterfield says we operate in the realm of natural law. The failure of the dream at level two is the experience of discovering our limitations. For example, my wife, Sandy, and I have two sons whom we love dearly. Much of their pain becomes our pain and much of their joy becomes our joy. We have dreams for our children, and of course these dreams must sometimes part company with these children as they grow into who they will be.

When our children were born we had all kinds of ideas of how we would raise them. It soon became apparent, however, that the children had their own personalities which would play a large role in shaping their futures. Our cat we have raised to be the pet we wanted it to be. Our children have grown to become themselves.

One experience which showed us our own limitations in affecting the lives of our children came when we realized that our oldest son was going to repeat third grade. Matthew was young for his class, chronologically, physically, and emotionally, and school had been a struggle for him from his very first day.

It is not easy to have a child struggling through school in our rather typical community where a great emphasis is placed on achievement. The norm around here is intelligent, high-achieving children, and it was difficult to face losing that dream.

We ran into the limitations of our dreams. We could not make our son into something he was not, so with the support of friends and the help of his teachers we made the decision to let Matthew repeat third grade. In the process we noticed something special happening. We shifted from concern for our plans to an awareness of his life. We found that by accepting our limitations, something could be done to break the cycle of struggle that was school for him. He is in a much better place in his life right now. There is a host of talents and gifts developing in him that just could not seem to blossom before.

This is really a small crisis. But really small is still real. It helped me to understand a realm of life which I could not control. On a very simple level this is what Butterfield labels the realm of natural law. At this level, recognizing the limits of life is recognizing another element of reality. That reality is a depth available if we are willing to trust letting go of the norm in order to find our own meaning. It is a liberating experience to give up a great chunk of egocentricity.

"Can any of you live a bit longer by worrying about it?" says Jesus (see Matthew 6:27, TEV). That is a good statement for this level two failure of dreams. William Sloane Coffin, Jr. says that as a stream only finds its depth when it encounters its bank, we only find our depth when we encounter our own limitations.[2] Letting

[2] William Sloane Coffin, Jr., *The Courage to Love* (San Francisco: Harper & Row, Publishers, Inc., 1982), p. 17.

go of the belief that I can control everything and trusting in the depth of life's gifts is a deeper kind of success. It opens life to newer dreams yet.

This brings us to level three in lost dreams. Here we are talking about the most difficult level of survival itself. Butterfield calls this the realm of providence. Here we simply cope. The advice given at levels one and two is trite at level three.

A family whose three-year-old son is struggling with a life-threatening kidney disease is at level three. For two years he has been in and out of hospitals constantly. Family members say that the chance to make simple decisions about their life is a luxury right now.

Another family, refugees from Laos, is at level three. I really do not know what struggles they went through before they arrived in this country. I do know that for two years they lived in a refugee camp in Thailand. For some reason the mother and two of the daughters wound up in a separate camp. One day Church World Service found sponsors for the family so the father and four sons and one daughter were told that they were moving. Forty-eight hours later they stepped from a plane in Gainesville, Florida, with a few suitcases and no understanding of English. Now they are separated by thousands of miles from a familiar land, the mother, and remaining daughters.

I thought of them and of the family with the sick child, and the words of the psalmist came to mind, "By the rivers of Babylon we sat down; there we wept when we remembered Zion. On the willows near by we hung up our harps. How can we sing a song to the LORD in a foreign land?" (Psalm 137:1, 2, 4, TEV). A family sitting in a strange hospital room on a long, lonely night, or a family thousands of miles from home must wonder how they could ever sing the Lord's song again.

Most of our lives are spent in levels one and two, planning for the future, worrying about where we will live, work, and follow our dreams. But there are times when all of that is gone. Freedom is hardly a word in level three and it is cruel to say that the experiences which people suffer at level three will somehow make them better people or instill in them a deeper freedom. No, this is a place where, like Job, with home and family destroyed, we stare across an empty breakfast table in stunned numbness.

The only answers for those at level three must come from those who have been there. Such an answer was shared one day by a man in our congregation who grew up in Korea. Richard offered this not as advice for anyone else, but as an experience of meaning for himself. When he was a teenager, the Communists were over-running his hometown, conscripting all eligible males for military service. Richard was hidden by his family in a crawl space under the floor for thirty days. In that place where he could not stand or exercise, wondering whether he would live or see freedom ever again, he experienced these words, "My grace is sufficient for you" (2 Corinthians 12:9).

"My grace is sufficient for you." Perhaps only when we are in level three do those words come through with the power they have to keep us alive. They are like a second wind for a life, a word which appears when all other words disappear. Other people who have experienced the depth of level three have shared this sense of meaning in times of serious illness, the loss of a loved one, the flight of political chaos, the terror of natural disasters.

Paul described the time when he wrote the words "My grace is sufficient for you" as a time of the most difficult pain of his life. He prayed to God three times that his infirmity be cured. He was not cured, but he heard the words, "My grace is sufficient," and it was.

Paul writes best when he speaks from level three. For when we pace the hospital hall at midnight, gather up belongings after the flood, hear a disconnected voice explain that hope is gone, another word is spoken. This second word is like an echo if in the silence we can tune our ear to it, it is a word of grace, love, strength from somewhere unimaginable. Butterfield calls this the level of providence.

It is easy to lose hope in the face of providence, for such experiences may seem to come from the hand of a malevolent fate. But from the edge at level three, beyond the clichés of levels one and two, a faith can appear which turns fate to a kind of destiny.

It is important to distinguish the levels at which we experience the loss of dreams. Level-one dreams lost take us into the power of human freedom. Level-two dreams lost show us the limits of freedom and the depth of life in contact with the laws of nature themselves. And level three is somehow beyond both of these; it is in a realm of providence, which moves from fate to destiny. In all three levels there is at least one common thread—to lose is to find, for when the myth-like qualities of the dream pass away, truth finds its voice and speaks with its deepest power and love.

Questions for Reflection

1. When have you experienced the loss of the "American Dream" of success and security? Did this give you a greater freedom?

2. At level two, experiencing limitations, and confronting elements of natural law, when have you encountered your limits? Did you discover a greater depth in the process?

3. At level three, beyond freedom, beyond finding depth in limitation, have you encountered a crisis where all that was left was grace? Did you sense the realm of providence moving fate into destiny?

4. How do the categories of freedom, natural law, and providence apply to three levels of dreams in your life right now?

4

How Do We Reach Out "When All the Laughter Dies in Sorrow"?

The following thoughts, written in poetry form, were triggered by the title of a poem by Kenneth Lasalles, "When All the Laughter Dies in Sorrow" (1968). I share a personal working out of faith at the edge in times of sadness and loss. What do I need, and what can I offer in times of pain?

When all the laughter dies in sorrow,
and a darkness seems to fall,
the words that once had meaning now fuzz and run into nothing-
　　ness.
I can feel that pain of emptiness take hold of my heart.
No matter what I try to do—eat, sleep, get up in the morning—
it is still there,
gnawing at my emptiness,
gripping my hopelessness.
It has only touched me lightly.
I can only imagine its full weight.
I have sat with people bound and locked by it.
I have watched as one by one well-meaning friends tried to lighten
　　the darkness with kind words.
But the words fell into nothingness, dying with the laughter.
I have tried the words for others and seen them fall.
I have worried over the words, wishing, hoping, thinking:
　　If I could just get them right,
　　they would work.

Then I remembered a time when the laughter died a small death
    in sorrow for me.
I found how wordy words can be,
how meaningless the talker's talk falls upon the listener
    who listens in sorrow.
My remembering was of my dear college friend who one night
    tried to take his life.
I remember the laughter of my day,
a day of love and plans for a beautiful future,
disappearing as the darkness of that night surrounded me.
The kindest words almost became the harshest
as many tried to step into the brink,
the gap where one person decided life
was not worth the struggle.
I wanted to speak the right words to Jim;
I wanted the right words to get me through this night.
But help did not flow, strength did not come
until the words ended,
until I listened, in silence,
until someone else shared
mine.

Our Bible's Job lost everything dear to him.
He cried out from his sorrow:
"A man dies, and that is the end of him;
he dies and where is he then?" (Job 14:10, TEV).
Page after page, sentence after sentence,
his friends
preach to him.
Their comforting mocks him.
Their consolation confounds.
The laughter of his life dies sorrowfully in the words of his friends.
They are no help.
I meet so many now,
like Jim, like Job, or like no one else,
just suffering, sorrowful, lost.
What can I say? "Through suffering God is refining us for greater
    things"?

"God offers you comfort, why still reject it?"
These are jokes, and cruel.
For when the deepest part of life itself is lost,
when a life is uselessly wasted,
when all you and I worked so hard to keep is gone—
Then what is the word?
When my wife's grandfather died,
I watched his wife of 53 years greet the friends.
Some helped.
Some did not.
Those who had to make their statements long helped the least.
The words made the room empty.
I felt the iron chain of sorrow grip her heart as I had known it grip
    mine.
What words could help her failing faith?
And then in a silent time of all of us together
I felt a strength growing among us—
a strength I've seen and felt before,
in hospitals, in homes,
right here,
a strength I have been unable to name in late night dark and lonely
    rooms,
which came and filled us there again with something,
something other than us alone.
A strength: it was
to be there
but be silent.
In those moments the silence overcomes the darkness
of just too many words.
For all the answers to all the sorrow do not fill that sorrowful void.
The answers of Job's friends did not help.
They just made his agony worse.
For what good is a reason for suffering if your wounds still burn?
What good is a reason for the pain of a child
if you still must face that small child's cries?
What good is a reason why a job was lost
if the emptiness of that unfillable day still stares across the breakfast
    table?

What good is a reason why a love no longer loves you
when you still reach out and there is no one to touch?
No, now is a time for something else.
Someday the whys must be known.
Someday a great amount of words must be spoken.
Someday there will be a chance to say, "It all makes sense."
But today, the day the laughter dies in sorrow,
I simply need to know
I'm not
alone.
The day your laughter dies in sorrow,
I simply need to let you know,
you're not
alone.
The day the laughter dies in sorrow,
and all the words and reasons that have given life its meaning
fall, drift, and pass into their fuzzy worlds,
let the words go.
Do not speak them to another.
Do not look so much to reasons for strength.
Instead know that in a quiet presence
God
reveals
not reasons for the pain or flood
of anguish,
but Godself.
And when someday my laughter dies indeed in sorrow,
and the worst I ever fear to lose is lost,.
this, I believe, is what I need to fill that night of darkness:
no great theologies,
no neat wise sayings to help me face tomorrow,
but the silent, present, loving God.
Strength,
for a moment at least,
to face the loss.
And I would also need a hand,
yours
to touch mine,

to be there as a sign
that through you God's hand holds me that moment
beyond the wisdom which now seems so sadly small.
And this too I would want to give to you,
when your laughter dies in sorrow,
a hand for God to hold you,
so that you could find
a beginning,
a sense that what was lost,
what you thought could never be found again,
is you,
and you
are found.

Questions for Reflection

1. Reflect upon a time when the laughter died in sorrow for you. What enabled you to make it through that time?

2. In that moment what did you fear losing the most?

3. In times of grief or sorrow what would you *not* want to hear from those who seek to help?

4. In such a time what do you anticipate you will need from those around you in the future?

5. A suicide attempt was mentioned in this chapter. Is this something you have gone through with someone near you? Was there a healing of this pain, and how did it occur?

5

Life After Death—How Do We Face This, Our Deepest Doubt and Highest Hope?

To walk at the edge of faith is to walk with an unsteady gait. It is unsteady because our feet touch different paths. Sometimes one foot is in heaven, the other on earth. One foot may walk the path of action, the other of contemplation. There is a rhythm in the walk of faith and if we lose the rhythm, it is no longer faith. Some days one step is much stronger than the other, but the rhythm must remain.

The culmination of that rhythmic walk of faith is in the question of life after death itself. Here one foot walks the path of hope; the other the way of doubt. In fact, when confronted with the Christian claims of Easter and resurrection, we face our deepest doubts and our highest hopes.

For the person at the edge, the doubt and fears of death are the dominant step. The claims of the Gospels—the empty tomb, the appearances of the risen Lord—are difficult to accept without doubt. But the other foot of hope swings into place. That step brings us to church on Easter Sunday. If life after death is our deepest doubt, then it is also our highest hope. It is in fact our last hope that this path holds the truth of the matter, that even in death all is well.

If we are unsteady in walking this dual path of doubt and hope, the Gospel of Matthew is equally unsteady in its walk right beside us. The step of doubt brings us to the crucifixion. It is a stark scene of despair. Crowds jeer at Jesus, tempting him again to save himself with one of his own miracles. The bandits on either side of the cross join in. No pleasant words from Jesus' mouth, no promise for the bandits, no forgiveness for the crowd are recorded in Matthew's Gospel. Jesus cries, "My God, my God, why did you abandon me?" (Matthew 27:46; TEV). This is the impact point of the step of doubt and despair: Jesus experiencing with us the absence of God when we need God the most. Then it is recorded that Jesus gave a loud cry and breathed his last. The sky goes dark at noon, the veil of the temple breaks, and humanity experiences its lowest moment.

Confusion follows. There is a strange story of graves breaking open and some people getting up and walking around. This is the traditional Jewish concept of resurrection, which Matthew includes, but it is not what he wants to tell us about resurrection. Plans are made, details taken care of, the body buried, guards posted. The darkness holds fast.

But there are two women who keep the rhythm going. Why they return to the tomb, we do not know. Is it sorrow or is the cycle of faith beginning to move toward renewal? The other foot so gently moves. This step of hope gathers its power. The women move with it, and from then on all creation moves, too. The stone is rolled away. An angel greets them. Joy and fear mix. The women encounter the risen Lord and then call the other disciples to go to Galilee as he asked. Hope is rising, but even in this, hope's clearest appearance, some doubted.

And that is what happens every Easter Sunday, or perhaps every day since that first Easter. We wake up with our doubts. We rise and in our own way we worship the power of hope by living our lives. That is the two-legged, two-stepped, double-path truth of the Easter message. Something happened and we are here, reading of faith, loving, worshiping, trusting that this is not a dead end. Because of this, the community that we call the church exists. No one can tell us more than this. I do not even think that those different people who were there on that first day of resurrection could tell us more. Even Matthew's account is short, not short and simple, but short and confused. Those first followers knew something happened and they would not give up. Today we can say, "He lives; he is with us. All is well and though we doubt, we will not give up. From our deepest doubts we can live into hope."

This of course is the claim of Matthew. Faith is only "worth it" if it is confirmed in life. And it is. It is confirmed in a child who goes through a time when all friends seem lost, or a hurt unbearable, or a crying feels as if it will never stop. In these times just the thought of school makes the stomach ache. Even pets don't understand. Then a new friend appears. The hurt heals. What seemed broken forever is glued, and everyone is able to laugh again. That is rising.

Faith is confirmed in teenagers. Everyone knows of those adolescent years which are unlike any other time in life. One year you felt good, looked cute, had friends, did well in school, and could talk to your parents. But overnight this is all lost. Parental communication is gone. Love goes bad. You don't grow, or you grow too much. You feel angry, alone, with nothing to believe in. All life seems to be waiting. The step of doubt hits hard.

Then you make it. Another year comes, and then another. You find the love you lost and the beauty that was hidden. You know that if you don't have it all together yet, you will nevertheless get it someday. You look at the person who has been there the whole time and say, "Don't worry about me. I'm going to be all right." The step of hope swings through. That's rising.

Faith is confirmed in college. There is a time in those years when you feel as if you are going crazy. Everything you believed in at home is pulled out from under you. Your roommate throws you out to have someone else in for the night. The brightness they said you had in high school is suddenly very dim amidst other bright lights. The love that promised meaning is gone. The path to the future that seemed so clear has dropped off the face of the earth. You could go back home. They love you there—that's clear. But that wouldn't do. It is the future that makes the present so scary. The step of doubt threatens all else.

But then, just when it seemed you were sinking beyond recovery, the other foot of hope finds a piece of solid ground to stand on. You wake up one morning. The sun is shining, and you have a sense that this is going to be a good day, a new beginning. You take that step. That's rising.

Faith is confirmed in the stories of adults. As adults you just forget that you will keep having the same stories, even though you are not children, teenagers, or students. You have your stories of relationships broken. Those dear to you have left. Parents have died, friends have moved, marriages have broken, children have grown. You have felt as if the middle has been ripped out of your body. You had heard it was possible to make it through such pain, but you didn't believe it. The foot of doubt came down with a loud thud and it rocked you to your bones.

Then one day, another day, you noticed that while the hurt was still real, the pain was not eating away at you anymore. You've lived long enough to realize that the other foot of hope was already swinging into place. That's rising.

If you look deeply into your life, you have faced your empty tomb. The center has held. Something has happened—a resurrection. The hope could not have risen without the depth of doubt.

Those are experiences of life, ways in which resurrections of hope spring from our deepest doubts. But the title of this chapter asked how we face our deepest doubt and highest hope, life after death?

I share here a dream, a deathbed moment, and a vision.

The dream was shared with me by a retired Lutheran pastor, the father of a member of our church. His name was Paul Erney. He spent a long time dying a painful death. We did a lot of talking about his experiences in small rural churches. He did not talk a great deal about dying itself. He was a man of simple faith and dedicated service. A few days before he died, he was so weak he could barely open his eyes. He whispered to me, "I've been having a dream. I was standing in the middle of a field shouting 'Hosanna.' It's funny. In a way I'm ready. I'm looking forward to it." Two days later he died.

His dream came to me with the impact of hope's highest truth. I didn't have the feeling of anyone trying to prove the truth of the resurrection to me. Instead I felt his rising and in turn my rising, and finally a rising for all.

The deathbed moment came two summers ago. The deathbed was that of my father, and like running to an empty tomb, I ran to him in his final moments of dying. We had shared the awareness and experiences of his cancer for five years, but struggling through the last year and months of his cancer was difficult for all of us. How do you say and do all the right things when you know your time is limited? I lived a thousand miles away. I received that phone call saying this was probably the end and by the time I reached him, he was in a coma.

At his deathbed, as I stood there trembling, trying to reach him through that veil of silence, I received a gift. In his silence he communicated to me a promise of love that outlives death and its fear. His dying was a time of sharing with me from his place in eternity. He showed me the bittersweet mystery of loving and letting go. I had spoken of such things before, but had never truly experienced them until this time.

Finally, a vision. Last year my wife's brother and his wife had a baby girl, born prematurely. Her name was Amy, and she died the day after she was born. My wife and I were with them during this time. Too stunned to speak, I had to listen. I have never experienced anything more painful than the death of a child. From that silence it was as if all the loved ones I had buried spoke to me, saying they would keep the baby in their love. This was the vision, that in love neither they nor this baby Amy would die. No higher hope could spring from any deeper doubt.

To walk at the edge of faith is to walk with the unsteady gait of one who has one foot on the path of doubt, the other on the path of hope. Living on the edge of life means facing the deepest doubts of darkness and despair. Only by encountering that pain can we then experience the vision of hope breaking through the darkness with its light. We walk the path of faith in rhythm of doubt and hope, or not at all.

Questions for Reflection

1. How do hope and doubt walk in rhythm for you?

2. How do you see hope springing from doubt in life's difficult moments?

3. What experiences of "rising" have you known in your life?

4. What have been the experiences of doubt and hope in moments of death and dying near you?

5. There is a Buddhist walking meditation in which you use the

rhythm of your footsteps as a means of opening the spirit to a new consciousness. In it you simply become aware of all the processes involved in taking each step and use that concentration to free your mind of distractions. You may want to use this walking meditation some time simply to be open to this experience of the rhythmic walk of faith.

6

How Can We Handle So Many Voices Calling for Commitment?

The next few chapters deal with a host of big issues such as abortion, capital punishment, and war. Just listing them can make me tired because they constitute a litany of guilt which can burn out even the most committed fighter for social justice. Before addressing these issues specifically, I want to share my own experience of being overwhelmed by issues, causes, and calls for commitment. That overwhelming experience did give me a framework for dealing with the many voices calling for concern. It did not solve the problem of burnout or commitment but it gave me a perspective as well as a measure of grace that I can draw on when I need an extra gift to see me through. It is important to have such gifts, for the issues continue, and they will not leave alone those people who believe in being on the cutting edge of love and justice.

My own experience is that social and political demands seem to run in packs. I can go for significant periods of time without too many disruptions to my life. Then all at once, it seems, there is an issue at the nearby prison; the question of abortion presents itself to me both publicly and personally; world hunger is in the headlines and at my doorstep; questions of war and peace polarize not only the world but the community in which I live; and I find myself in conflict with a close friend.

The following is something of a waking dream. It recurs in different forms whenever I get overloaded. It reminds me of what I should already know. It is only a story; it is not literally true (I think).

The story is this. I am going to church, ready for morning

worship. I find a person, a young man or maybe a boy, sitting at the door. He won't let me in. He does nothing to stop me. I just cannot get around him. He is a familiar street person. I have seen him before, and he wants a handout. These street people arrive regularly in Florida, ahead of the latest cold front which chases them down from the North. They have the same sad stories. Somebody stole their wallet. Their car broke down on the way to Tampa. They're out of gas, and hungry children are waiting outside.

I have a system for deciding who gets money from me and who does not. It is basically an alternate feed. I gave money for a bus ticket to a father and son the last time I was hit this way, and I'm pretty sure that it was a con. Today I'm going to say no. The director at our community referral center has told me over and over again that she cannot help us organize community care if we keep throwing away money that could be spent on real needs.

I am ready with my "no" when I look at the face again and realize that I am quite mistaken. It is not a man off the street at all. It is someone I know quite well. We communicate, but you can't really call us friends. It always seems that the relationship has potential. He is one of those persons one would describe as an "almost" friend. At times he's a pompous bore, and at other times we seem to be on the brink of closeness. It just never quite clicks, so I am waiting for him to straighten himself out. Until then I don't have energy for him.

As I move closer, I realize that it isn't he at all. This person looks up at me, and I catch the eyes for the first time. It is a woman, a very hungry woman, and with her is a very hungry child. This is the most desperate case I have ever seen. I want to feed her and her child immediately, there is no question about it, but something reminds me of the many times I've neglected the issue of world hunger because of its complexity. The old paralysis stops me from acting as I stare at these empty faces.

You can see what is happening in my story. All the faces I try to ignore in my daily life recycle in front of me. To the faces already seen add the victims of war, economic disaster, depression, all those for whom I argue my way out of responsibility through some rather well-developed intellectual gymnastics, and you have the picture of faces at the church door.

I make up my mind to go around these faces when these words come from one of the faces, "If you are about to offer your gift to God at the altar and there you remember that your brother [or sister] has something against you . . . go at once and make peace with your brother and then come back and offer your gift to God." This happens to be the text for this Sunday's sermon, the troublesome words of Jesus in Matthew 23-24, TEV.

I am not much for self-appointed prophets quoting Jesus to me, so I tell this last person, whoever he is, that I am doing fine with my sisters and brothers; and in fact I am on my way right now to worship with them. He says that this is not enough. I go on about my need for the renewal of singing and praying so I do not overburden myself with goals I cannot meet. He tells me that is a worthy goal, but it will never work.

I am just stalling. I already know this. After all, he is right; so instead of going to worship, I go home. I decide to be ready the next time. I give money to the street people, listen to the overtalkative friend, and barriers seem to be falling. I can't find the woman with the hungry child, but I do recommit myself to the cause of world hunger. I make a financial contribution and cut down my intake of beef.

I feel much better. Taking hold of these issues gives me an inner peace I had not known before. I am glad those faces stopped me from going to church. It should be much more meaningful for me to worship now, so I go back to church.

I cannot get in. All the same faces are there with a not-so-gentle revelation of the superficiality of my actions. They point out the host of sisters and brothers I have not yet begun to face with peace. Now I get the point. I am still engaging in tokenism. I need to go deeper and reach many more people. I know I can do it.

I expand my area of concern and reach more deeply at the same time. I don't just give money to transients; I work with a group at the soup kitchen to help them get their lives together. I spend time with people with whom I now have only a shallow relationship. I devote my skills to alleviating world hunger. I continue to offer myself to people in prison, refugees; you name it.

But I am not terribly welcome in all these places with all these people. My skills do not always match their needs. Individuals are not as receptive to relationships with me as I had thought. But I will not give up. I am ready for the long haul and I go back to church, confident now that I am making peace.

The faces are still there. The sad boy is still sleeping in the streets. The almost-friend still carries on his lonely banter. The hungry woman still has her hungry child. New faces continue to appear, faces of people I had made commitments to long before these sad faces began appearing. These are faces of family, friends, co-workers whom I am abandoning for my newfound social awareness. Nothing is working.

The last face appears again and asks, "Have you made peace with your sisters and brothers?" What more does he want? A person can only do so much, and I am doing just that. As I begin to defend myself, I see my own face in the crowd blocking the door.

It is not a face of peace. It is the face of one who wants a simple solution to all this conflict. It is a face that glosses over people to get issues straight. That face, my face, does not show an ability to make peace with someone full of hate or loneliness. It is not a face which looks as if it can stick with the roots of injustice or the causes of hunger.

The voice repeats, "If you are about to offer your gift to God at the altar, and there remember that your brother or sister has something against you, go first and make peace with your neighbor, and then bring your gift to the altar."

I back away. I cannot escape the faces. I feel as if I am on the edge of a large, dark pit. Even the church is denied me. I know the words are true and right, but I do not see how I can make peace with all these, my brothers and sisters.

One last time I return to the church door. The faces are still there. The one face of kindness calls me to peace again. I see this face and the face of my own emptiness.

Suddenly a knot in my chest unties and my heart breaks open in prayer. Old words rise from who knows where, "Lord have mercy." New words flow from distant dreams, "I'm falling God, into distant darkness.

I thought I could love them all

playing a game of how great I am
putting away all the problems of the world.
I want your help
to touch people, feed the hungry, shelter the homeless,
be a friend and love those dear.
I cannot,
alone.
I need your light in my own darkness."
    As these words flow, another face returns, which says simply,
"Yes.
Light, spirit,
love may arise.
I am with you, we share the struggle,
you are mine."
    The faces part. I can worship again. It is grace.
    That's my story. It has travelled with me for years, returning
regularly. My conscience is needled and I see new needs before me.
I try to meet the new challenge, seeking first to do it all myself,
and I invariably fall on my face. There in that stumbling place,
God reminds me, sometimes gently and other times with a little
more force, that I cannot do it all. Neither can I give it up altogether.
We are partners somehow. When I recognize that I cannot do it all
but through the grace of God neither can I give it up, there is a
sense of being embraced by the holy.
    I offer this story because the causes ahead are not just issues.
They are in some way the faces that stand before the door. They
call us to make peace with them before we seek to fill our spirits.
But to take them on alone, is to fall rapidly into despair.
    We are called to hear the issues, see the need, and know that we
cannot solve the problems of the world any more than we can
make peace with all our brothers, and sisters. That in itself is a
discovery of the spirit. When we accept our limitations in making
peace with our sisters and brothers, we experience grace. This grace
is a cycle of seeing, stumbling, and then rising again which repeats
itself over and over again.

Questions for Reflection

1. If you had to make peace with those with whom you were angry before you brought your gift to the altar, what faces would you see?

2. What would those faces say to you?

3. How would you reply?

4. Where is your altar? Is it a place of rest, challenge, release?

5. What word of reconciliation might you hear at your altar after having confronted these faces?

7

When Do You Hold and When Do You Fold? A Question of Faith

Perhaps the real question of this chapter is the role of faith in times of change. What is the call of faith in an era when the Moral Majority rises up with surprising popularity, when a new wave of political conservativism challenges the existing ways of meeting the needs of the poor and disenfranchised, and when suddenly one who thought liberalism meant looking to the future is now frantically hanging on to the past? What is faith in such an era? Kenny Rogers hit on a good answer in his song "The Gambler," in which he says that we have to know the difference between when we should hold and when we should fold.

Let me explain.

There are people who hold, no matter what. My uncle once gave me a good example of the logic of hold, no matter what. My parents were born and raised in the wheatland of central Kansas. I spent every summer visiting there as a child. One particular summer we were wrestling with the decision of what kind of car to buy. I wanted my father to buy another Pontiac because I liked the old one. My dad wanted a Buick. This is where my uncle stepped in and told his story. He said that one of the great debates he witnessed annually in Kansas was "Which is better, Ford or Chevy?" While the argument was never permanently solved, it was once summed up by a man who proclaimed, "Fords are best. I ought to know. I've never driven anything else." That is the mentality of one who holds, never folds, no matter what.

I had a little more trouble coming up with an example of the opposite extreme, one who folds as soon as things are looking bad. My difficulty comes, as I now see, from the fact that this position is much closer to my own. If the opposite of the person who has never driven anything but a Ford is one who's never bought the same brand of car twice, then it's me. Perhaps I listened to my uncle too well, because I not only switch makes every time I buy a car, I have a tragic tendency to buy cars in the first model year they are produced. The make of my worst car is really irrelevant, and since I am not familiar with libel laws, I will not identify that car other than to say that its manufacturer smartly sidetracked the public by suggesting its commonalities with a cute, furry, hopping animal.

Each of us has our blind sides, our tendencies to hold or fold too soon. Mine may well be folding.

There have always been two schools of thought on whether faith meant holding or folding. The "Hold" school saw faith as a firm foundation, a rock of certainty in a sea of change. That rock was easily identified with traditions of the past. On the other hand, the "Fold" school saw faith as a window to the future, a call to openness, receiving the promise of new futures in the dawning of tomorrow's kingdom. This latter school has been typical of religious liberalism in the late sixties and seventies.

My preference has been for the future. Faith for me has been looking for the ways God breaks in with the new, the creative, and the unknown. This is my faith at the edge. It is as the writer of Hebrews says, the assurance of things hoped for, the conviction of things unseen. I liked the litany of faith in Hebrews 11 which held up Abraham in his journey to a new land, Sarah willing to hope for a baby far beyond a time for reasonable hope, and Moses' mother who hid her son in the bullrushes for a future task yet unknown.

My own litany of faith developed.

Faith meant reaching ahead for peace in Vietnam.

Faith meant blacks and whites sharing life together in schools and open communities.

Faith meant worshiping with guitars and dancing, sharing and laughter.

Faith meant trying something other than killing people

with the death penalty to show that killing people was wrong.

Faith meant finding a way for our country to feed the hungry and house the homeless.

Faith meant liberation from stereotyped sex roles.

Faith meant an economic vision of shared resources where everybody had enough because no one had too much.

That's what I held to. And I knew when to fold. I did so eagerly on the Apostle's Creed, stuffy churches, the Republican Party, archaic religious language, outdated sexual rules, structured education, and the like. But there is a new era of concern now, a new political consciousness. Conservatism is a reemerging trend in government and religion.

Now, it seems, my faith which came to me so readily as a call to the future, to fold on the old ways, has become a call to hold, to hang on to the concerns of the past. One by one, programs for the handicapped, the environment, mental health, housing, hunger, are being dismantled. Instead of being a prophet who is calling people forward to new and uncharted experiences of faith and care, I find I am calling people back to a time when faith meant care.

I wonder, am I just a tired old knee-jerk liberal, unable to evaluate circumstances and situations according to their own merit? Am I like the farmer who drove a Ford all his life and therefore thought nothing was better? Suddenly the causes put forth by my own denomination, which once stirred me for their courage, are sounding a little too familiar. I am glad some institutions still care about the social arena, but deep in my heart I feel a certain emptiness in it all. In the liberal cries for social justice, there seems to be little room for a relationship with a loving God on a personal level who makes this love of neighbor dynamic, an experience of a center in a moving life.

I am discovering places where I have to hold as I have never done before and fold as I've never done before. It was easier when the formula boiled down to this: "Fold on the old; hold on the bold." But that's a formula, not faith.

To know when to hold and when to fold is to be grounded in a faith which is a spiritual bridge to God and neighbor. In the classic formula of H. Richard Niebuhr, faith is a call to love and serve both God and neighbor. It is a triangle connecting the self, God, and neighbor, and no single line of that triangle can be broken for it to remain faith. Liberals have too often folded on the line to God. The conservatives have too often folded on the line to neighbor. In this triangle there is never a time to fold on either.

Where does this leave us? First, we have to examine the core of our faith. In that faith there are some principles we must never give up. Jesus gives a good summary of those principles the first time he stands to speak in the synagogue. He takes the scroll and reads from Isaiah, describing how the spirit of the Lord calls him to preach good news to the poor, liberty to the captives, sight to the blind. Jesus says he is called to set free the oppressed and announce that the time has come when the Lord shall save his people (Luke 4:16-21).

This did not bother his hearers too much until he reiterated that he was the one the passage spoke about and the time was now. The crowd then ran him to a cliff at the edge of town and were about to throw him off. Now the theme of this book is life at the edge, and Jesus shows us again that there is a time and place to come back from the edge. He turned, faced them squarely and walked back in from the edge of the cliff. He retooled his ministry, gathered a community of supporters around him, went to another town, and softened his message with parables and healings.

Second, therefore, liberal religion in America may have to recognize that we have gone as far out on the edge as we could go. The result is that we have left a vacuum of moral leadership. We have forgotten how difficult change is. We have neglected the heart. Groups affiliated with the new religious political right, like the Moral Majority, have sensed the need and filled the vacuum. There is a time here to turn and face our critics. Often the only way to discover the blind side of our own theology and ideology is by having it confronted by a challenging and competing point of view. Our rival sibling often provides a mirror to show us who we are.

Third, we have to look again at the heart of what we stand for. We then have to separate the heart of what we believe from the strategies for accomplishing it. This is a distinction made by Peggy Shriver, as she describes the difference between the moral calls of our faith and the ways they are being carried out.[1] For example, concern for needs of the poor is a call of faith which is at the heart of Christianity. Meeting that need with food stamps, says Shriver, is a social strategy, one step removed from the essence of faith. Liberals accuse conservatives of not caring about the poor because of their opposition to food stamps. Instead of this kind of recrimination, it would be better to identify the concerns we both share at one level and then see how we can work out the best strategies to meet those needs.

This is one way out of the current impasse between those on the right who seem to want to dismantle every program of social welfare and those on the left who do not want to admit that there is any waste, inefficiency, or counterproductivity in such programs. I have served on the boards of enough community agencies funded with federal and state dollars to acknowledge that a good amount of that money is wasted. I also know that cutting out those programs without workable alternatives would permit the suffering of the mentally ill, the poor, abused children, and the impoverished aged to rise to intolerable levels. I must be willing to fold on outdated strategies and willing to hold on concern for victims of society in a way that can engage those with whom I disagree. To know when to hold and when to fold is to link the love of God and neighbor in such a way that the principles of faith can blend with the realities of the current situation.

Sometimes being on the edge has meant going with the flow of whatever new winds were blowing. It is time for a change. I do not necessarily want to be like Bob Dylan, going from born-again protestor to born-again Christian just to stay on the edge. It is time to examine where it is that we can hold fast to what we believe without losing the ability to dialogue with society.

Jews have held fast to the authenticity of their tradition and respect for practices like the faithful observance of the sabbath. Mennonites and Quakers have held fast to a commitment to peace, no matter what persecution or ridicule they have suffered for their moral imperative. Episcopalians and Lutherans have held fast to the beauty and integrity of liturgy. Baptists have held fast to the

---

[1] Peggy Shriver, "Conflict in the Christian Family," *Christianity and Crisis,* October 5, 1981, p. 264.

importance of biblical instruction and individual conscience among American Baptists, and personal renewal among Southern Baptists. The United Church of Christ has held fast to the importance of well-informed commitment to the social concerns of society as well as a continued openness to new forms of truth. It is good to have some arenas in which we just will not fold, others where we easily let go, and a host of others where each decision must be made anew every day.

How then does the knowledge of when to hold and when to fold affect our personal lives, beyond the struggles of society? We are reaping the whirlwind of the storm of cultural upheaval in personal growth, life passages, midlife crisis, sexual liberation, sexual role change, divorce, new stepparents, new stepchildren, and job uncertainty in a volatile economy. "Every hand's a winner, and every hand's a loser," says the "Gambler." Not every new idea is good, and at the same time the good old days have some elements which were good only because they were left behind. It is not a time to retreat to the fortress of yesterday or abandon all that is past to plunge into the chaotic battle of tomorrow. Instead, it is a time to accept a bonding with the heart of God who can hold you when everything around you is folding. For if our life is grounded in anything, it is not just the ultimate goodwill of humankind. Humankind is too often what has done us in. Our lives are grounded in a God who values a sparrow, just as God values you. It is a God who calls forth love not only in God but in God's children, to whom God has given birth in creation. Sometimes this God appears like an old gambler, sitting next to you on a train ride home from some horrible failure.

Jesus stood up in the temple to speak, Nazareth being his hometown. He gave them the words of Isaiah and to those words he would hold forever—good news to the poor, sight for the blind, freedom for the oppressed. The hometown crowd all nodded their heads in approval. But when he said, in effect, "The time is now and I am the messenger," they ran him to the edge of the cliff and tried to throw him over. In a way, he knew when to fold. On another day he would hold to his principles at the expense of life, and in the holding gain them both.

The old gambler on the train ride says, "Every hand's a winner and every hand's a loser." That may be a little extreme. But God works best in extreme cases, if you think about it.

Questions for Reflection

1. When was a time you held fast to what you believed and were glad of it?

2. When was a time that you "knew when to fold" and found healing and hope in a change of attitude?

3. What was the difference between the situations of #1 and #2?

4. In the continuum below, the point on the extreme left represents one who never changes, never gives up the ship, knows "Fords are best, I've never driven anything else." On the far right is one who folds at the first wind of change. Mark an X where you would place yourself.

always holds	holds 50% folds 50%	always folds

   a. Are you comfortable in the position you marked?

   b. Where is your blind side?

5. What are some guidelines that would help one to determine when to hold and when to fold?

6. In terms of current social issues, what principle will you hold to, no matter what?

7. In terms of current social issues, where are you willing to change (fold), especially in terms of social strategies to carry out your commitments?

8

How Do We Balance the Question of Personal Morality and Legal Rights in the Abortion Debate?

The question of abortion is one of the most painful issues before us for many reasons. It is painful on a personal level, for most of us have had to deal with it somewhere close to, if not in, our own lives. It is painful on a public level because the religious right has claimed to be pro-life in opposing abortion and has labelled those who disagree either pro-abortion or anti-life. It is painful on a moral level because it is a dilemma which is not a simple choice between right and wrong.

When I graduated from Yale Divinity School in 1969, I had received a good intellectual background on the pros and cons of abortion. I had read Roman Catholic doctrine which viewed the purpose of all sexual activity to be the creation of a child. Thus the Roman Catholic church stood against abortion, birth control, and masturbation, considering them all sins. Catholic theology viewed the fetus as a full human being from the moment of conception. Protestant theology was rather obscure at the time but generally allowed for the morality of abortion in extenuating circumstances. Legally, the procedure was a crime. Practically, thousands of abortions were performed every day, safely if the client had money.

The year after I graduated, abortion was legalized in New York, the state neighboring my church in Connecticut. Almost immediately, I was counselling a young woman wanting an abortion. The academic arguments suddenly seemed very vague. My own ambiguity faded as I heard her story and it became clear that if I did not help her, she would probably have an abortion illegally. I contacted a new group called the Clergy Counselling Service for Problem Pregnancy. This group had direct contact with a safe, inexpensive clinic in New York City. The young woman went there.

I became one of the counselors with the group and began dealing with women facing the dilemma of unchosen pregnancy. My role was to help them talk about their feelings about being pregnant and look at their various options. I never suggested abortion, but if the woman made that decision, I referred her to the New York clinic.

I remember the nineteen-year-old college student from Taiwan who was frightened and embarrassed. If her parents discovered her pregnancy, they would send her home. This had been her first sexual experience and everything about it was painful. There was a forty-five-year-old Roman Catholic mother of four whose youngest child was sixteen and whose doctor had told her that she was beyond childbearing age. Now as a mature woman with a grown family, she sought an abortion. I saw women of all ages, from high school through adulthood. I dealt with strangers and I dealt with people very close to me. Perhaps out of the whole group of women I saw, one took the situation casually. For everyone else, it was a soul-searching experience.

The arguments in the abortion debate are familiar. The traditional argument against abortion is that of Roman Catholic canon law echoed by Protestant anti-abortion forces. Since the fetus is a human life from the moment of conception, according to this point of view, it has a soul and is entitled to all the rights and protection of any human life. To take that life is both morally and legally wrong. This is why anti-abortion forces are not satisfied in letting abortion be a matter of personal moral choice. They consider it murder, and that is not a moral choice recognized by a society based on law.

This ethic, which sees life beginning at conception, viewing no difference between actual and potential life, and allowing no place for consideration of the situation of pregnancy or the motivation of the action terminating pregnancy is a rule ethic. It is based on absolute principles. In this rule ethic, right is right, and wrong is wrong.

The opposite of a rule ethic is a situation ethic which looks at each moral decision based on the issues of that given situation. What is good is decided according to the factors of that situation and cannot be applied beyond that experience. Neither wrong nor right is applicable beyond that moment.

I believe that the best ethical decision making is based on both principle and situation. A total rule ethic is often too rigid, and a situation ethic is often too flexible to give meaningful guidelines in a difficult moral dilemma. Significant moral challenges occur when good and evil are not clear, in principle or situation, and they have to be balanced in a struggle of competing calls for justice and love. In those situations we recall our best principles and apply them according to the uniqueness of a given situation.

The single argument that abortion should be prohibited on the basis of the absolute right to life of the fetus as a full human being is not a sufficient moral basis legally to prohibit abortions. There is a difference between biological processes and human life. There is a well-recognized principle in society distinguishing between potential and actual life. Our heritage of common law recognizes that circumstances can determine the morality or criminality of any given act.

I believe in the morality of contraception, and on any given occasion when a couple decides to use a contraceptive, they also decide that a life which could potentially come from this union will not be. They have distinguished between potential and actual life, and that is a moral choice.

I believe that all women should have the legal right to choose an abortion. I believe that every child has the right to be born through a decision to be wanted. Therefore the issue of birth control is closely tied to the issue of abortion. There are often two layers of concern about abortion. One is as it concerns us personally. We may want the right to make the decision ourselves and have legal access to abortion if we so choose. On the other hand, we worry about those we consider the "others," who are perhaps having their second or third abortions and are simply using abortion as a form of birth control. For those others, removing legal access to abortion seems to increase both the prospect of illegal abortion and the misery of unwanted, abused, and underprivileged children. Our moral concern over the abuses of abortion should be directed toward better sex education, which would include the proper use of contraception.

It often seems that those who oppose abortion also oppose instruction in the use of birth control as well, and this is perhaps an even more important legal battle to fight. Sometimes I fear that the anti-abortionists want simply to punish people for behavior they consider immoral. That is not a proper basis for ethical thinking or public policy.

Here are the places I believe we can stand with moral integrity on the abortion issue. First, if the scriptural injunction, "judge not that you be not judged" (Matthew 7:1) applies anywhere, it is here. Abortion has touched practically every American family in one way or another. There are those who have faced an unchosen pregnancy and decided to follow the pregnancy through to the birth of a child. There are those who have chosen to terminate such a pregnancy.

There is no way to say that one decision makes the other wrong. Even the history of the rule ethic which anti-abortionists use to support their claims is one of mixed claims. There has seldom if ever been unanimity within the church as to when life begins. Aquinas believed that the fetus was "ensouled" or formed as a human life forty days from conception in a male, eighty days in a female. St. Augustine did not believe the soul existed at conception, and within the church the date of the beginning of human life moved back and forth from conception to a time as late as the ability of the fetus to survive outside the womb.

The current Roman Catholic position on this issue became official in the nineteenth century. There is still difference of opinion within the Catholic church on the beginning of life, and Protestant leaders also have virtually no agreement on when life begins. For a rule ethic to be acceptable, it needs greater consensus than this. We are thus forced into examining factors at hand in making the choice regarding abortion.

Here are some guidelines for that choice. When we see human life as distinguished from biological processes, we see a difference between potential and actual life. For a period of time the personhood of a fetus is potential. During that time a person is free to use the God-given freedom of choice to decide if that pregnancy should come to term. Here all the situational elements of that decision are relevant. What is the condition of the family? What will the economic impact be? What is the genetic history? What was the circumstance in which the woman was impregnated? What is the health of the woman and what risk does childbirth present? These situational issues all have a rightful place in the decision-making process. They should be balanced against the equally serious realization that the potential for life of the fetus is also precious, and that termination cannot be taken lightly.

The degree to which others should be involved in the decision making is difficult to assess. The role of the father in determining the decision depends largely on his situation. Fathering is more situational than biological and the degree to which he should have a right in this issue is certainly relative to the history of his relationship with the woman. The potential father could after all be a rapist, a casual acquaintance, a longtime faithful lover, a husband with a history of care and nurture, a husband with a history of abandonment or abuse or, in the case of incest, the father of the pregnant woman. The male role in moral choice is dependent upon his link to the situation.

Finally, the decision is often very private for the woman who must make it. It is not taking the place of God to make the decision to abort or carry the fetus to full term. God has set humankind and nature in radical freedom. God does not take poison from our mouths or set us in speeding cars bent on destruction. God calls us to make choices to be fully human. Refusing to choose is refusing our divinely created humanity.

Given all of this, abortion is never a simple situational decision. It is still related to the principle that we are dealing with potential life. The closer that potential moves toward actuality, the more serious must the reasons be for its termination.

None of us knows completely the mind of God. Our vision is not entirely clear, but we know that God calls us to act, even when our knowledge is partial and our vision unsure. Whatever we do is subject to brokenness, and here is where God calls us with compassion and forgiveness.

Here is a time for prayer, to open oneself to God, light, and the personal strength available in times of crisis. Answers may not be simple nor directions clear. Moral choice is not profound when good and evil present themselves clearly. Real moral choice occurs when decisions must be made between greater and lesser evils.

If you do not face this dilemma yourself, you may be called some day to walk with someone who does. This is the time and place to walk the extra mile of compassion that Jesus speaks of (see Matthew 5:41). If you face this difficult decision yourself, then realize that God does no less for you than God calls you to do for another. God walks that extra mile with you, sometimes in the form of another, and sometimes in God's own gracious presence.

Questions for Reflection

1. In what circumstances do you believe that abortion is a valid moral choice?

2. In what circumstances do you believe an abortion to be immoral?

3. In what circumstances do you believe abortions should be legal?

4. In the continuum below, the point on the extreme left represents total support for freedom of choice in regard to abortion. The point on the right represents total opposition to abortion under any circumstances. Mark an X where you would place your current belief regarding the morality of abortion.

abortion as a matter of free choice	opposition to abortion as an option

5. What are the principles supporting your position?

6. What elements of circumstance and situation inform your position?

7. What is the danger for excess in your position?

8. How would you deal with the dilemma of an unplanned pregnancy in your own life? In the life of someone close to you seeking your advice?

9

Where Is the Cutting Edge of Justice and Mercy in the Death Penalty?

I live in Florida not far from the state prison in Raiford where John Spenkelink was executed. For the last two years I have gone once every month to that prison to visit with Douglas Raymond Meeks, an inmate on death row. Ray, as he likes to be called, has been on death row for eight years. He is twenty-eight years old.

Ray grew up in Marks, Mississippi. After visiting Marks in 1962, Martin Luther King, Jr. was moved to organize his famous march on Washington. The poverty of Marks, it is said, made Martin Luther King, Jr., cry.

Ray left his hometown to work in a fruit-packing plant in central Florida when he was nineteen. He sent most of his money home to his mother and sisters. When the season was over, he left for home. In the rural panhandle area of Florida, Ray's car broke down. He went to sleep in his car by the side of the road. When he awoke, he found a sheriff pointing a gun at him. Ray spent the next two weeks in jail without being charged. When he was released, his car still impounded, some of the people in the black community took him in. A few weeks later a convenience store was robbed and the clerk murdered. A survivor identified Ray as the gunman.

I honestly do not know if Ray committed that crime. The person I have come to know is a gentle, quiet person. He loves to draw and play basketball. We send him art supplies so he can draw whenever possible. He gets to play basketball once a week when he is permitted to go outside. He enjoys jigsaw puzzles and books about animals. Whether Ray is guilty or innocent, I will continue to visit him and do what I can to prevent his execution.

Why? In 1976, Florida Governor Reuben Askew signed the death warrant for John Spenkelink. His imminent execution just a few miles from where I live made what was once an academic argument very personal. My latent opposition to capital punishment was driven to the surface. Here is the background of my thinking.

Statistically no one has been able to prove that the death penalty is a deterrent to crime. In fact some argue that the notoriety which goes along with the death penalty actually attracts people with both a death wish and a desire for fame. After the execution of Gary Gilmore, there was a brutal double murder in a convenience store in Utah. This pattern is not uncommon.

Our ability to deny death is just about the strongest defense mechanism we have. A criminal does not commit a crime thinking he will be caught. If caught, he does not believe he will be convicted. If convicted, he does not believe he will receive the death penalty, and if he is sentenced to death, he does not believe he will die. For every hundred murders committed, generally one person is convicted and sentenced to death. The murder rate is higher in the death-penalty state of Florida than in any nondeath-penalty state. The death penalty proclaims the message that life is cheap and killing can be justified.

Another reason for opposition to the death penalty is the totally uneven way it is administered. The white, wealthy, well-connected are not sentenced to die. Less than 3 percent of the current 200 persons on death row in Florida are there for murdering a black person. Almost all 200 inmates are poor and/or black.

America has a fantasy that our judicial system is better than it was before 1972 when the Supreme Court abolished the death penalty, ruling in Furman vs. Georgia that executions were carried out in an inconsistent and discriminatory manner. We have a picture in our minds that mistakes like those dramatized in the story of "The Scottsboro Boys" or "To Kill a Mockingbird" do not happen any more. We assume justice works more precisely today.

This is not true. The courts are as capricious as ever. For example, I recently attended a clemency hearing, Florida's last review in capital cases. There I heard the case of a man who had stabbed a woman in a barroom brawl. She was taken to a nearby hospital where she was left on a stretcher untreated for two hours. She died from suffocation caused by her swollen windpipe before she was given any medical attention. Her assailant was convicted of first-degree murder and sentenced to die. He now sits on death row. Since then, the victim's family has sued the hospital for negligence. Medical testimony indicates that had the victim been treated with a simple tracheotomy, she would have survived. A $50,000 payment in damages was made by the hospital to the family of the deceased. The defendant is no hero, but does he deserve to be on death row? By the time it is decided whether this case is legally first-degree murder, will the defendant still be alive?

Our worst criminals, Sirhan Sirhan, Richard Speck, Son of Sam, are not executed. It is the nameless, hapless defendant who is.

Those of us who hold to the sanctity of life are called unrealistic in believing justice can be done without executions. I say it is the people who think our system of justice can ever be perfect in imposing the death penalty who are unrealistic. It is estimated that at least 5 percent or one out of every twenty persons executed has later been proved innocent.

We live in an imperfect world, and one of our imperfections is our legal system. But the death penalty is the "perfect" solution. There is no room in it for error. What is done is done.

Perfect justice restores what has been taken. In the case of a murder, perfect justice would restore the life which had been destroyed. The taking of a second life as punishment does not bring justice. Instead it perpetuates more injustice. It is impossible to do justice by murdering a murderer. And the norm in all the Bible is that where it is impossible to do justice, we are called to love mercy.

It is argued that it is too expensive to keep these people in prison for life. In reality it may be less expensive to keep a person in prison for life than to go through all the legal appeals and court cases necessary to bring a person to death.

All that is left as a reason for the death penalty is our desire for vengeance. Vengeance is a natural human emotion but not one which is acceptable in either the Judeo-Christian tradition or in our legal system. I believe that when the state kills a human being in our name, we have brutalized ourselves. We have made murder legal and acceptable. We have traded our reverence for life for the right to kill, perhaps one, perhaps one hundred persons a year in the electric chair. It is cold-blooded evil to decide on an hour of death, march and strap up a human being to a chair, and pull the switch.

There is nothing in the Judeo-Christian faith to justify this. There are no executions committed by Christians in the New Testament. The Christian story is in fact the story of those executed by the state.

The death penalty exploits the sadistic forces which exist in human hearts. Shortly after Spenkelink's execution, the Jacksonville, Florida, police made up 20,000 T-shirts with a picture of the electric chair and the words "1 down, 133 to go." (There were then 133 people on death row). The T-shirts were sold out in a week.

John Spenkelink, thirty years old, was convicted of killing a man who had sodomized him and forced him to play Russian roulette with a loaded pistol. Spenkelink was sentenced to die. His first death warrant was scheduled in 1976. Three days before the date of execution, the order was stayed.

A number of us went to the prison the night of his scheduled execution to stand in silent vigil, reminding ourselves and the community how close the state of Florida had come to executing John Spenkelink that night.

We stood outside the Florida State Prison again on Tuesday night, May 22, 1979. Robert Graham was the Governor now, and he had scheduled Spenkelink to die on Wednesday morning at 7:00 A.M. Various groups concerned with the death penalty had gathered for this vigil. It was a disorganized affair. It reminded me of the great feast described in Luke where all the invited guests made excuses and the castoffs of society were called to take their places (Luke 14:15-24). That dinner must have looked like our vigil of tired, dirty, sometimes hysterical, often shouting, angry people. Jesus said that those were the people of the promise, but I found myself wishing they would maintain as much dignity as Spenkelink himself.

Different speakers crowded around a bullhorn. One stands out in my memory. He was Rev. Joe Ingles of the Southern Coalition of Jails and Prisons. After Joe said a few words about the case, someone asked him to say a prayer. It appeared that Joe looked around rather reluctantly and then prayed for John's life. It seemed hopeless to me, even to pray. Then at 12:30 A.M. word came that Supreme Court Justice Thurgood Marshall had issued a stay of execution. This was followed by another longer stay from the Federal Circuit Court. We all took prayer, persistence, and presence more seriously. If the execution were not carried out by Friday noon, the warrant would expire and the process would have to be redone. Where there was life, we remembered, there was hope.

We went home, continuing our cautious hoping. On Friday, May 25, at 2 A.M. I was awakened by a call from John Talbird, one of the organizers of Citizens Against the Death Penalty. The warrant had been vacated and the execution was scheduled for 10 A.M. that day.

My wife, Sandy, and I drove to Raiford for our third vigil. The confused band of protestors was still leaderless. Some beat on oil drums and shouted. One small group seemed overly emotional to me until I realized that they were the mothers, sisters, and wives of men on death row. There was a black minister, Greg Thomas, who managed to gather most of the crowd into a circle. Within the circle we sang, prayed, and read Scripture. Outside the circle, they watched. At 10 A.M. all fell silent.

We heard nothing until 10:20 when Spenkelink's brother-in-law walked by the fence saying, "He's dead but they won't let us in." Then the witnesses to the execution were driven by, and we knew it was over.

Tom Feamster, an Episcopal priest from a nearby parish who had ministered to John Spenkelink for the last three years, came by to talk with us. Tom had not been allowed to be with John during his last hours. Florida statute at that time did not allow a death-watch prisoner to have clergy with him or her. It only allowed the clergy of his or her choice to witness the execution. Spenkelink asked Tom to witness his execution, which he did, reading the Beatitudes until the time of death.

Tom told us that John would not have us pray for him in this moment but for ourselves, our state, and our nation which could do such a thing as this.

There seems to be no other answer. We work and pray for men

and women of courage to stand against the death penalty. The arguments are well known. It is time to decide and act.

As time seemed to be running out on the warrant for Spenkelink's execution, Florida Attorney General Jim Smith said that Spenkelink's lawyers would probably just keep finding sympathetic judges to beat the warrant. Smith, however, beat the lawyers. And this is what it has come down to, the last lawyer to get to the last judge in the last hour. John Spenkelink lost the race. This is a far cry from justice. There are over 200 persons on death row in Florida today and more than 1,000 nationwide.

It is time to act on the courage of our convictions. Dante said that the worst places in hell were reserved for those who tried to preserve their neutrality in a time of crisis. If we believe the death penalty is wrong, then we must act. To say nothing is to give consent to the status quo, and the status quo is the death penalty in thirty-five states.

Action is keeping after our legislators. In Florida, these are the same people who have already committed themselves to the death penalty, but we do not give up. Action is continued education, organization, petitioning, letter writing.

Personally, I have chosen to visit at least one death row inmate, Ray Meeks, regularly. By seeing Ray I cannot forget that this is a human issue, not just a political debate. Ray does not talk about his legal situation as June Rice and Steve Stitt, volunteer lawyers, continue to argue Ray's case in state and federal courts.

Ray does not give up hope. "You can't ever give up hope," he says, "that's all you got." We hope together.

Today I received a call. Governor Robert Graham has just signed a warrant for Ray's execution, scheduled for three weeks from today. Ray has been transferred to a cell directly across from the electric chair. I believe that the execution will be stayed. By the time you read this, he or someone else may have been executed.

It is a time for prayer. Once, when asked how to pray, Jesus told the story of a widow banging on the door of a crooked judge (Luke 18:1-5). She had no legal rights, but eventually the judge responded to her plea. We keep banging on the door of mercy, for how else could God act without violating our freedom?

Eventually, I believe, we will be rid of the death penalty. We will follow the path of virtually all other civilized nations and find it unacceptable. But how long from now will that be? Will it be in time for Ray or another whose name we do not yet know? The questions rest heavily on those at the edge.

Questions for Reflection

1. In what situations do you favor the use of the death penalty?

2. In what situations do you oppose the use of the death penalty?

3. In the continuum below, the point on the extreme left represents total opposition to the use of capital punishment. The point on the right represents total support of capital punishment for serious crimes. Mark an X where you would place your current attitude toward the use of capital punishment.

---

against   for capital
capital punishment   punishment

4. What elements of your faith support your position on the continuum?

5. Where is the blind side in your position?

6. What circumstances might cause you to change your position, moving it either to the right or left?

7. In what ways might you act upon the commitments reflected here?

10

How Can We Find Meaning in Genesis Today?

In 1925, in Dayton, Tennessee, a biology teacher named John Scopes was brought to trial for reading the theory of evolution to his sophomore science class. In what became known as the "Monkey Trial," William Jennings Bryan argued the case of biblical literalism in behalf of the state against Clarence Darrow for the defense. While the state won, wide publicity clearly gave Darrow's argument the edge. Bryan, embarrassed on the stand by Darrow, died a few days after the trial. When the trial ended, it was widely proclaimed in the media as the "last hurrah" of fundamentalism.

Fundamentalism, the belief that all biblical record is literally true and equally inspired by God, clearly is not dead. People such as I, however, have forgotten about it. Main-line and liberal church leaders have become somewhat lazy in biblical work and sloppy in the defense of both faith and freedom of speech. Fundamentalism, however, is alive, organized, and active in the current campaigns of the new religious right to reinstate the teaching of creationism in the public schools. Laws have been enacted in Louisiana and Arkansas to require the teaching of creation science. Laws are pending in more than fifteen other states for a similar mandate. I share here some of the homework I have had to do as I have been confronted by the proponents of teaching creationism in the public schools.

Basically, the creationists are arguing against evolutionists on their own terms. Scientific creationists begin with the assumption that the world was created by God. This makes them creationists.

They claim to have scientific data supporting this view, which in their view makes them scientists. They consider the average biology text, which argues that the available ingredients in the primeval ooze that was the ancient earth merged to form a primitive cell, to be illogical and naive.

The scientific community, on the other hand, acknowledges that no one really understands how these primitive nucleic acids and amino acids could have assembled spontaneously to form a living cell. It is almost impossible to conceive of the complex blueprint of enzymes which translates into the DNA pattern for life as happening by chance.

Dr. Gary Parker, a biologist at the Institute for Creation Research (ICR) in California, says that all of us can recognize an object created by a man. He holds up a Dr. Pepper soft drink can and says that all the natural reactions, chance, and time in the world will never result in a little blue can with "Dr. Pepper" written on it. Through the same reasoning he argues that human beings could only have come to life through the intelligent design of the Creator. You can deduce God from God's mark on human beings just as you can deduce Dr. Pepper from his mark on the can.

The creationists find the holes in evolutionary theory and replace them with strict fundamentalist dogma. They argue that the earth was created by God about ten thousand years ago. They admit it may have taken more than six days. Adam and Eve were created by God and we are their descendants.

Duane Gish of ICR has footprints of dinosaurs from Texas which seem to indicate that man and dinosaurs lived at the same time. But his real evidence comes from the Bible's assertion that man and species of animals were all created at the same time.

If other arguments are presented to say that fossils prove that life existed prior to human life, creationists argue that either the devil put those fossils there to confuse us or that God was perfectly capable of making a perfect world, which would include fossils (presumably [a] to throw off the faithless, [b] to have something to put in museums, or [c] to have a source for fossil fuels. But now I'm getting cute).

Strict creationism can't have a billion-year-old world. When Bishop Usher, a sixteenth-century scholar, added up the ages of everyone in the Bible, he came up with the creation of the world occurring at 4004 B.C., October 23, Monday, I believe. Fundamentalists will stretch this to 10,000 rather than 6,000 years ago, but no more. Cosmologists argue for an earth that is billions of years old, not thousands.

Creation scientists are not asking that the Bible be taught in public schools. Instead they argue that evolution is a theory, as is creation science, so teach them both. They claim to have scientific data currently excluded from classrooms. They are arguing in some cases that evolution itself is a religion, therefore equal time should be given to creationism.

They provide texts which present a thin layer of scientific data over a strong base of the Bible. They believe that evolution is the cornerstone of secular humanism which is in turn responsible for most of the moral ills of modern society.

What do we do with this? I believe that Genesis is not a science book. It is a book of faith. Read through Genesis, chapters 1 and 2. We have here two contradictory stories of creation. Genesis 1 is actually the newer of the two. It is known as the Priestly source, or just P. It is called P because it was written down by the priests of the temple sometime between 500-200 B.C. This was a time when Israel had fallen and its people were in exile. Jerusalem had been invaded. The priests used this old story of creation to give Israel's faith some order when all external order had collapsed. We can identify the Priestly source, which runs through most of the first five books of the Bible, by its use of the name Elohim for God, here translated simply as "God."

This P source draws on very old images, primarily a Babylonian epic called Enuma Elish, which means "When on High." This epic tells of how the god Marduk Bell grabbed up Tiamet, the goddess of chaos, to form the earth. The Israelites demythologized this story to reflect the work of one God who had no biological relationship to chaos, as did Tiamet. The story in Genesis 1 introduces the concept of creation not by struggle, but by word. It is very sophisticated for the biblical story of creation to understand God to say, "Let there be light" and there was light. The Babylonians would have had their gods swinging fire at each other for eons before they ever got a spark.

At a time when Israel had lost Jerusalem, experienced the crumbling of its faith, and perceived no purpose in its existence, the priests took the oldest accounts they could find in the stories of their people and offered them to say, "You are a people with dignity, created in an orderly manner out of chaos. The sabbath is God's day and you must cling to it, and each of you is the most beautiful being God could create. You exist in His image."

Israel saw the world's existence as paralleling its existence. God called Israel into being in Egypt and led the Israelites forth into new life. In the same way God called the world into being. God who created once, continues to create. "In the faith of Israel," says B. Davie Napier, "creation always *is*."[1] That is the truth of Genesis 1, a truth that has carried faithful people through centuries of struggle, through the holocaust of World War II, and into the present. Creation continues. Creation always is.

Scientifically, Genesis is a mess. It has plants being created before the sun. It pictures a universe with water above and below the earth and a dome holding up the heavenly water until it rains. The story has nothing to do with geology. It need not have its six days of creation reconciled with anybody's theories of cosmogony, because it contradicts itself within, and it is contradicted again in the next story.

Genesis 2, beginning with the second half of verse 4, is a different story altogether. It is actually the older of the two stories, written about 900 B.C. Israel was still in a rather stable situation at this time. The story is more a folk tale. It is known as the J source because the word for God here is Jahweh, translated "Lord God." In this story the first work of creation is man (not mankind, but man), molded from the dust of the ground and given life by the breath of Jahweh. Jahweh is a human-like God, friendly, walking in the garden, changing God's mind.

It's an interesting story, but not terribly relevant. Why did it survive alongside the more sophisticated Genesis 1? Napier suggests that while Genesis 1 gives meaning to Israel's existence, Genesis 2 gives expression to the essence of God's relationship with individ-

[1] B. Davie Napier, *Song of the Vineyard,* Harper & Row, Publishers, Inc., 1962, p. 50.

uals.[2] The J source understands that God forms life by giving us breath. We are united by God with the soil and the air we breathe, and this is a relationship we fall into and out of for life. The fall of Adam and Eve in the Garden, by the way, never had the status of original sin that it received in the Christian church. The J story tells of four ways the relationship between humanity and God was broken. First was the eating of the forbidden fruit, the refusal either to live up to our created goodness or accept our limitations. The second way was Cain's killing of Abel, which reflects our tendency to destroy our brothers and sisters. The third fall was the flood, a time when humanity got so bad, God decided to wipe out all but one faithful family and try again. After the flood God promised Noah never again to destroy everything that lives and made the rainbow the sign of this covenant. The fourth fall was the Tower of Babel, where people lost their ability to speak with one another as a result of building great towers to the sky.

To recall the great mythological impact of the Genesis stories is important, not just to be ready for the fundamentalist argument the next time it comes up at a school board meeting, but for your own faith as well. Genesis is not just for biblical literalists. You have a heritage in Genesis which speaks to you today as well. This heritage calls you to remember that your story is, in a way, the same as the world's story, and the world's story is, in a way, the same as the story of the people of God. There is in you the created image of God. The power of God moves over you as it once moved over the waters. The chaos of the world, like the chaos of your life, is stilled by the creative power of God in you. That chaos, nevertheless, remains in the world and in you. It is channeled, molded, restrained, and renewed by the loving God who calls you through a living Word. This is your heritage, a heritage of faith and freedom. It is threatened at this juncture of history by the same powers that wanted to force this country into narrow fundamentalism in 1925.

To force Genesis into a framework of scientific creationism does injustice both to science and to faith. To reject scientific creationism is not to reject Genesis. Rather it is to free the workings of the spirit to continue to yearn toward creation today.

[2] *Ibid.,* p. 51.

Questions for Reflection

1. What elements of the biblical account of creation in Genesis are important to you?

2. What elements of evolution are important to you?

3. What is your position regarding the teaching of "scientific creationism" in the public schools?

4. What principles—biblical, theological, and constitutional—go into your answer to number 3?

5. What is the potential blind side of both a strict prohibition against teaching scientific creationism and of establishing it alongside evolution in the public school curriculum?

11

If We Honestly Wrestle with the Arms Race, How Then Do We Hope?

If you have ever contemplated the prospect of nuclear holocaust, then you know how difficult it is to hope in the face of the mushroom-shaped cloud. I am going to address four elements of dealing with the nuclear arms race. They address the enormity of the problem and lead finally to hope. The first element is the awareness of just what and with whom we wrestle in beginning to deal with the arms race. The image used here is that of Jacob wrestling with the stranger. The second is a question of what wounds in our lives express themselves in our need to participate in the arms race. Third is the nature of the call to be peacemakers. Finally is the affirmation that in facing the pain of our current nuclear age there is the power to hope.

With Whom Do We Wrestle?

In Genesis 32:22-32 is the story of Jacob who encounters a stranger in the night. Rabbinic literature interprets the stranger in four ways—the self, sister or brother, enemy, and God. I have found that this understanding of Jacob is a good point of reflection for wrestling with the arms race, for in it we wrestle in part with ourselves, our sisters and brothers, our enemies, and with God.

Imagine for yourself the struggle of peace as the dark night of the soul. Like Jacob, you are about to cross over a river of truth into a new awareness. In your wrestling, you are confronted with a vision, a stranger who stops you from going farther.

In this kind of night, truth washes over you in such a way that you do not know whether you wrestle with God, your own psyche, a rival sibling, or some nameless, fearsome, force of evil. You see a figure before you, struggle with it, and refuse to let it go until you have understood its word of truth.

The best current image of this wrestling is that of Luke Skywalker in the film "The Empire Strikes Back." Here Luke enters a dark cave as he seeks the secret of "the Force." His time in the cave is his time of learning for the difficult tasks that lie ahead of him. In that cave he encounters the vision of his archenemy, Darth Vader. Vader represents all that Luke stands against. Luke unleashes a mighty blow and knocks off his enemy's helmet. Then the unexpected occurs. When the mask splits, Luke Skywalker sees his own face.

Each of us has a shadow side. Seldom can we see it ourselves. Often it is the enemy who reveals it to us. In this revelation we recognize that the enemy whom we thought to be the other person, out there, is indeed very close, if not within us. The face of the enemy gives us a glimpse of who we are, shadow side and all.

We wrestle with the arms race, the horrors of war, in much the same way. Like Jacob, like Luke Skywalker, at some point in the wrestling we come face-to-face with the enemy. As long as we see that enemy as an object to be hated, a thing to be destroyed with whatever weapons we have at our command, it eludes us. Like the stranger in the night, it will not be contained. But when this monster of nuclear war itself tears off its mask and shows us our own face, it wounds us as the stranger wounded Jacob.

One wound it inflicts is the loss of innocence. No longer can we blame the other side for the evils of war. The enemy resides within us. "We have met the enemy," as Pogo used to say, "and he is us."

The struggle does not end there. Continue the vision for yourself. Other faces appear. It is often a rival sibling, a competing ideology who shows you an element of truth. To wrestle with something as powerful as the arms race, you must struggle all the night long. If you stay with the struggle, you may extract a blessing and a healing. You may be wounded on the way, but you may also travel on. The vision finally will bless, not curse you. There is a promise that your eyes will be opened to see self, rival, enemy, through the eyes of God. A new path is now opened for a final vision.

At the end of the night, as dawn is breaking, what was enemy, self, and rival turns and tells Jacob that his new name will be Israel, for he has wrestled with the vision of humankind and prevailed.

The stranger who wounds, now heals and promises a new future. There is a possibility for hope beyond all the evidence that went before. Like Jacob, you are to hold on to the vision until the day breaks and the figure with whom you wrestle offers a blessing.

This is a place to begin. I believe this vision opens our eyes to the deeper realities of what we face. I keep it with me, for when speakers who are either pro-military or anti-war begin labeling enemies for me, I am reminded of my own face behind the enemy's mask. When I seek to close my ears to the claim of rival ideologies, I remember that it is often this competing point of view that reveals truth to me. And finally, when I struggle with the fearsome unknown, I discover my own shadow and in turn my God.

What Wounds Live in the Arms Race?

Our inner and outer worlds are connected. The world in which we live is a mirror of who we are. Here is one picture of our world as a nuclear arsenal. Right now there are approximately 50,000 nuclear weapons in the world, divided roughly in half between the United States and the Soviet Union. I tried developing a visualization exercise to imagine the mutual dismantling of this arsenal. I thought it might be helpful to visualize the United States and Russia, each dismantling one nuclear missile, in turn, every other day. When I added up this process I discovered that at a rate of one a day it would take us 136 years and 8 months to dismantle the world's nuclear arsenal. That's what we are up against. We literally cannot see a nonnuclear world in our future. How did we come to this?

One way of hoping is in looking to the origins of our current dilemma and then moving from there. To do this we might well ask what wounds exist in our lives that have caused us to create this world. What wounds in us now live in the nuclear arms race?

Consider this for yourself. It is not a rhetorical question. It is a good question to ask of friends and leaders. Something hurting within has caused us to build personal defenses which then become

departments of defense. And our current technological capability
now enables us to destroy the world with our own defenses.

Wounds are pain and hurt we carry within us that are somehow
beyond the realm of traditional terms like forgiveness. They are
not something to be argued away.

What are the wounds in your life that express themselves now
in the need for a national nuclear defense? Are they part of the
horrors of World War II, Korea, or Vietnam? Are your wounds
personal, the result of having to learn how to fight as a child? Have
you been wounded by political terror of the right or left? Has the
violence of our culture destroyed your trust in humankind? Do
you bear the wound of the first time someone really hit you, or
perhaps the last time? Is your wound simply one of fear? Is your
wound a loss of pleasure in life itself?

Think about such wounds. I am really a novice in this and I
believe this is a good field to be explored. It seems that we develop
a warlike language of the arms race from these wounds. We live
over and against our enemies. We live our personal wounds into a
national hurt which seeks security by promises of invulnerability
and super strength.

The wounds have caused us blindness. We cannot see our planet
without the nuclear arsenal we have created. Even if we were to
begin dismantling that arsenal day by day today, we could not see
136 years into the future for its completion. We are blind to a nonnuclear future.

Therefore, imagine your wound as blindness. Let this be your
wound whether you consider yourself a liberal or conservative,
hawk or dove, romantic or realist, pacifist or militarist. Wounds
are to be healed. This is what the gospel is about, the healing of
wounds.

The stories of Jesus contain many images of healing. A good
picture of healing for this blindness is the story of the blind beggar
Bartimaeus (Mark 10:46-52). I want to follow the story of Bartimaeus in a way offered by Walter Wink, a New Testament professor, who shares a lively way of becoming involved in the biblical
process of transformation.[1] I participated in a Bible study with him
at the Kirkridge Retreat Center in Bangor, Pennsylvania.

[1] For a more detailed explanation of his method, see his *Transforming Bible Study*
(Nashville: Abingdon Press, 1980).

Wink suggests that we let ourselves enter the mind of Bartimaeus, and that is what I am going to ask you to do. Understand first who Bartimaeus is. He doesn't even really have a name. Bar means "son of." Timaeus is a family name. He is simply known as the son of Timaeus. He may have had some awareness that Jesus performed healings, but according to Mark, these healings were not great public events.

Jesus and his disciples had come to Jericho, and now they were on their way out.

Now let yourself be blind Bartimaeus. Who knows how long you have been blind? You may have a coat, your mantle spread out before you to catch the money people throw your way. You have heard something of this Jesus. He is now coming your way, and you hear the crowd approaching. What do you expect Jesus will do for you? How will you get his attention?

You think that the approaching crowd must be Jesus and his entourage. You cry out, "Jesus! Son of David! Have mercy on me!" You are making a political statement, a claim for which Jesus will finally be executed. He has been telling his followers to keep this kind of language quiet, so they run over and tell you to quiet down. But you are blind. You have nothing left to lose, no way to see your way clear to the rest of your life. You shout again, "Jesus, Son of David, have mercy on me." You hear the crowd stop. Jesus is saying something to his disciples, and they come. "You're in luck," they whisper. "He wants to talk to you."

Here is your crucial decision. You are a blind beggar, beyond embarrassment. You throw off your coat, perhaps your only security, jump up and go toward Jesus.

Jesus asks, "What do you want?" He forces you to identify your need and no longer remain passive. After all, there are many kinds of things that could be provided for the blind—money, job training, a place to live, food. What do you want? And you, blind Bartimaeus, reply, "Teacher, I want to see again." Say it from your blindness. Say it out loud. Say it with the boldness of a plea for life. Hear yourself shout, "I want to see again!"

"Go," says Jesus, "Your faith has made you well." He speaks these words to you as well as to Bartimaeus.

Our blindness to peace is like that of Bartimaeus. We sit on the sidelines in the darkness. We feel powerless. We are shouted down in our first cry for peace.

And then we shout again. We refuse to let our cry for peace be silenced. A moment comes, the right moment, and we leap up. We have to speak what we want, clearly. We must expect a miracle.

Such moments come. But first the deep wounds must be addressed, admitted. And when we face the horror of our blindness, for neither you nor I can see a world without nuclear holocaust on the horizon right now, we leap up and call for a miracle. We want to see.

There is a promise of healing in experiences such as this. We begin with exploring our wounds. We risk asking for their healing. Faith may grant us sight, and with that sight we may walk the now seen path of peace.

The Call to Be Peacemakers

The following chart has been developed by Jim Grier and Sharyl Green of the Norwich, Vermont, Peace Center and is used with permission. It is a graphic illustration of what we face. This chart illustrates that one does not have to be a pacifist to recognize that the magnitude of the world's current nuclear arsenal is insanity.

Nuclear Weapons Chart

1. World War II lasted six years, killed more than 50 million people, and affected almost every country in the world. The combined firepower, including the two atomic bombs we dropped on Japan, equalled 3 million tons of TNT or 3 megatons. On the following chart a single dot represents 3 megatons. The firepower of World War II is represented by the dot in the center square.

2. Right now, there exists in the nuclear arsenals of the United States and the Soviet Union a total firepower of 18,000 megatons, represented by all of the dots on the chart. (The chart has 120 squares with 50 dots in each, totalling 6,000 dots.) About half of the dots belong to the United States and the other half to the Soviet Union. Between us we have the destructive capacity of 6,000 World War IIs.

3. In 1977 President Carter said that one Poseidon submarine could destroy all the large and medium-sized cities in the Soviet Union. Each Poseidon has 200 nuclear warheads on it, with the total destructive capacity of three World War IIs. This is represented by the circle in the upper left-hand square.

4. A Trident submarine carries 24 megatons or the equivalent of eight World War IIs. See the lower left-hand corner circle. Our first Trident was built in 1981. The Navy plans another one every eight months, so you can increase the circles on the chart accordingly.

5. What percentage of bombs would be used in a limited nuclear war? Ten percent? Cover 12 squares with your index finger and see how many still exist. This 10% could destroy about 70% of the ozone layer in the Northern Hemisphere and about 40% in the Southern Hemisphere. As a result, animal life could soon be gone; sunburn could destroy most remaining life.

What we now face is the potential destruction of the entire earth. We have the power to reverse the very act of creation itself. We threaten not only our own lives, but the lives of all generations yet unborn. Our excuse is a policy of deterrence, a policy which is a failure even if it is successful 99.9 percent of the time.

It is inevitable that unless something is done to reverse our present direction, weapons in place will at some time become weapons in use. Nothing we seek to preserve and protect—freedom, faith, or life, here or in Russia—would survive a nuclear holocaust.

Leon Wieseltier writing in the *New Republic* (January 1, 1983) says that the deterrence we seek must now be linked with disarmament. To deter the use of nuclear weapons, we must begin to dismantle them. We can dismantle nuclear weapons for years before we begin to approach any sort of vulnerability. Wieseltier suggests that if we made a significant voluntary gesture to take apart some of our nuclear weapons, we could begin a change of heart for both Americans and Russians. It would cost us virtually nothing in terms of security but profit us much in morality.

I share this at this point to show that when we begin looking at the end of the arms race, there are paths which lead to hope. I will return to this later. But the question which arises in everyone's mind at this point is "Can you trust the Russians?"

Yes, William Sloane Coffin, Jr., said, you can trust the Russians to disregard a large measure of human rights. You can trust the Russians to be hard on dissidents. You can trust the Russians to act horribly in international diplomacy. But there is something else you can trust the Russians to understand, the horror and death of war.

When Russians marry in Moscow, the first place they visit after the wedding is the cemetery, for virtually every family has someone buried there who died in World War II. Twenty million Russians died in that war. The Russians have known the plague of death in war in a magnitude unique in the twentieth century.

You can trust the Russians to act no better than we, which in itself is a challenge to raise our international morality. But can you trust the Russians to see the horror of nuclear destruction? The answer is that we have no choice. Both the Russians and we now have a greater enemy than each other, the common threat of nuclear destruction.

The wound that the Russians and we share is a new and growing awareness of the common threat which our nuclear might poses not only to each other but to the whole world and thus ourselves.

Where does this leave us? There is a beautiful story in 1 Kings 19. In this story Elijah has spoken as a prophet, speaking the word of peace against the word of death. For his efforts he was run out of town. Jezebel is hot on his heels, threatening to kill him. Elijah runs to the wilderness and says, "It is too much Lord, take away my life." He lies down under a tree, exhausted.

How many times have you felt this way on your journey of faith?

Then an angel bakes Elijah a cake. By a gentle word and a cake, says Robert Raines, Elijah's flight is turned into a pilgrimage.[2] This can happen for you, says Raines. An angel of mercy can turn a flight of fear into a pilgrimage of peace.

Elijah then goes to a cave, a place of shadows and spirits, like all places of change and spiritual growth. It is protective. It is frightening.

In this place that both terrifies and sustains, God calls, "Elijah, what are you doing here?" Elijah cries that he alone remains and is scared. He protests that for all he tries to do that is just and right, people try to kill him.

And behold, the LORD passed by, and a great and strong wind rent
the mountains, and broke in pieces the rocks before the LORD,
    but the LORD was not in the wind;
and after the wind an earthquake,

[2]Remarks made at Kirkridge Retreat Center, Bangor, Pennsylvania, January, 1983.

> but the LORD was not in the earthquake;
> and after the earthquake a fire,
>   but the LORD was not in the fire;
> and after the fire,
>   a still small voice.
>
> —1 Kings 19:11-12, RSV

"What are you doing here Elijah?" The question repeats like the chorus of an endless song.

Today the question comes to each of us, "What are you doing here?"

In a world where death threatens the existence of all in a nuclear holocaust, "What are you doing here?"

This call goes forth to you and me, right now, just as it went forth to Elijah. When the world is hot on our heels and we run for our lives, that call comes not in the earthquake, wind, or fire, but in the still small voice of God saying, "What are you doing here?"

When you realize that you may respond to that call with clear direct actions and prayers for peace, your journey turns from a flight of fear to a pilgrimage for peace.

There are visions we may now see, with our eyes newly opened. We may envision the end of war as an international institution, just as our parents in faith envisioned the end of slavery. We can begin simply, with daily prayers for peace, simple conversations with our friends, staying educated on the arms race, a letter a month to a legislator. Our flight becomes a pilgrimage, and we may share this message with others in the same way.

You may share this message with others, too. The message of peace, while difficult to face at first, may be like the cake the angel left, now offered to a frightened world. You may be the one to show another sister or brother human being the way out of the horror of our nuclear madness by offering him or her a chance to visualize the safety of peace. If you do that, you become an angel of peace yourself.

Our Pain Is Our Promise

In each of the previous examples—Jacob wrestling with the angel, the blindness of Bartimaeus, the flight of Elijah—the initial confrontation with the fear the biblical person faced was difficult. In each initial look at the nuclear madness of our world, the first glance is painful and difficult. However, from facing the pain before them, these biblical characters experienced power. The same is true in our nuclear dilemma.

Out of curiosity I asked the teachers in our church school to have the children make two lists. On the left side of the paper they were to list what they saw ahead for themselves in their own lives. On the right they were to indicate what they saw ahead for the world.

That's all I asked for.

The list of what's ahead for personal lives is just delightful. The youngest children affirmed that they would simply grow up. One even said, "I'll grow up and be twenty years old." Another said, "I'll grow up and be a famous singer—in high school!" There was one simple "I will live."

The older children were more specific, with clear visions of the American Dream. Computers were high on a lot of lists. One fifth-grader even gave the specific brand, memory capacity, and designated disc drive. I do not wish to have fun at their expense. They had beautiful dreams of growing taller, playing football, getting married, travelling, buying cars, raising pets, and living their dreams.

On the right side, as they looked to the future, there was a startling uniformity. They all saw nuclear war. And if you wonder at the success of the current crop of films dealing with extraterrestial creatures, it is to a figure from another world that they look for some kind of intervention to save the world.

I asked for the list from the young people I know for two reasons. First, I had heard of a study by the Educators for Global Responsibility which indicated the pattern followed by children. I quite frankly was skeptical of the pattern and wanted to check it out around me. Our young people conformed to the pattern.

Second, many times we say that we do not want to speak about our concerns over nuclear war around our children because we do not want to upset them. They are already upset. They live with the threat of nuclear destruction. If we deny this awareness, we contribute to the schizophrenia already rampant in our existence. By schizophrenia, I mean the awareness we all carry with us of the threat of nuclear war coupled with a life-style that denies the nuclear threat daily. Denying something which they know is real makes people a little crazy.

I share all this in order to say that in facing the pain of our nuclear dilemma, we discover our power. Our capacity to feel pain for the world is the promise of our ability to turn the world around. Our pain is our promise.

Joanna Macy says that in facing the pain of our nuclear dilemma, we discover our power. Our capacity to feel pain for the world is the promise of our ability to turn the world around. Our pain is our promise.[3]

Our problem in finding hope is that we deny our pain. We live with a split life, an awareness of nuclear terror coupled with a life-style that pretends nothing has changed. Because the world lives this way, it is difficult to convince people that by facing the prospect of nuclear holocaust, they are in fact participating in an act of hope.

Why won't we face the pain? Pain is viewed as dysfunctional. Millions of dollars are spent in America to mask pain, rather than listen to its call for healing. Since there is no pill to erase the world's pain, we repress it. A nation that can feel pain for others is considered weak. We may even believe that feeling pain for the world might equal loss of faith in a loving God.

The first step toward mental and spiritual health is to acknowledge our fears. A positive act of hope is to help one another acknowledge and name those fears. Pain for the world is normal. In fact it is a testimony to sanity.

Joanna Macy also said that to find power in pain, we must approach power metaphysically.[4] We have traditionally thought of power in Aristotelian terms. We consider as real only material substances. That which passes between them—feelings, beliefs, needs—is less real. Substances resist infringements from the outside. Power equals defense against what is outside.

But there is another way to look at reality. Instead of reality being made of separate things, each needing a piece of a fixed amount of power, we may see power as flowing through all life.

[3] Remarks made at Kirkridge Retreat Center, Bangor, Pennsylvania, January 13, 1983.
[4] Ibid.

Lewis Thomas in *Lives of a Cell* speaks of membranes which transform the energy which passes through them. Our power exists in the way we transform the existence which passes through us as membranes of meaning.

An article in *Newsweek* (February 7, 1983) described the incredible complexity of the brain. Neurons enable the brain to function by allowing energy to pass through them. One scientist, *Newsweek* reported, called the brain "an ungodly complex system" because he could not separate its many functions. No, it is a "Godly beautiful" reality, a membrane which functions by the powers which flow through it. The life of the brain exists in synapses between neurons.

Our power is the power of openness to let life flow through us as energy flows through our brains. Such is the power of peacemaking. Power does not lie in winning an argument or a war. Power does not lie in laying another burden of duty on another. Power is the freedom to identify pain and free it to promise. Our pain comes from the same source as our power, our ability to feel fear, hope, love, and joy.

I love the passage from Isaiah, "They shall beat their swords into plowshares and their spears into pruning hooks" (2:4). Our weapons of destruction are created from the same source as our instruments for nurture and growth. Isaiah continues, "Nation shall not lift up sword against nation, neither shall they learn war any more." Those words are on a banner in our church. Pictured at the bottom corner of that banner is the classic symbol of the peaceable kingdom, the lion and the lamb.

Someone once said that the lion may lie down with the lamb, but the lamb will not get a lot of sleep!

There is a wariness we now carry with us. Our children live their dreams with the nuclear shadow always present. But none of us will discover the power of the Word of God to transform our war-torn lives into the vision of the lion and the lamb until we envision, as have our children, the mushroom-shaped cloud.

Hope is not the same as optimism. It has been said that the optimist believes this is the best of all possible worlds and the pessimist fears he is right. Hope is something deeper and higher than optimism. The beginning of hope is the pain that washes over you when you become conscious of the power the world has to destroy itself. Let that pain rise within you. Feel the chill of the shadow that hangs over your children's lives as well as yours. Feel for a moment the terror that you may be the last person to see the people around you alive. Meditate upon the nuclear cloud annihilating everything you love.

Then let that vision be the beginning of your hope. As you hear the cries of creation, you will also hear the songs of hope. Small gestures of trust emerge as signs of power. The energy robbed by repressing fear is released to power. Open your life to a message of peace and it will come to you. It has long been waiting.

Throughout the Bible, from Jacob wrestling with his stranger, to Isaiah's visions of suffering, to the women who found the empty tomb, people whom God calls first see the potential for destruction that life holds. Then right on the heels of despair comes a vision of hope and a call, "Whom shall I send, and who will go for us?" (Isaiah 6:8).

To those who answered, "Here am I, send me," miracles of hope were offered.

I am no Pollyanna. I know that we are up against not mere flesh and blood but, as Paul said, "principalities and powers" (Ephesians 6:12). I look, as did Bartimaeus, for a healing of the wounds that have made us blind.

The hope that arises is a strength to envision a world in which the world does stop its nuclear arms race. And though the problems are immense and the time frame seems to be forever, I believe we can envision the gradual dismantling of the world's nuclear arsenal. Through the eyes of faith, we may envision peace in a world no longer on the brink of destruction. We may envision billions, now spent on the weapons of destruction, channeled to food and nurture. We may envision a world in which we have understood that our greatest enemy is not Russia but that together the world's common enemy is nuclear destruction.

It took such a vision of faith to see the possibility of democracy in a world which had never known such a form of government. It took such a vision to see a world without the institution of slavery. It will take such a vision to see a world united in a common awareness of the threat of nuclear extinction.

Blind eyes see in faith. There is no simpler hope when we wrestle with the arms race.

Questions for Reflection

1. In the continuum below, the point on the extreme left represents a position of pacifism, the opposition to all wars. The point on the right represents military security, a position which believes that international security can and should be maintained by military strength and war when necessary.

---

pacifism   security through
                                                                        military strength

Mark an X on this line where you would place yourself.

2. Do you need to change that X in terms of the advent of nuclear warfare?

3. How is your position informed by tradition in terms of theology and ethics, and how is it informed by the current political situation?

4. What wounds within you need a strong national defense?

5. Picture your wound in a way that makes sense to you. Take a few minutes to focus on that wound. Relax, breathe deeply. Now bring this wound to a loving, divine being for healing. You may picture that divine being as God, Jesus, or a glowing light. Let that loving entity embrace and heal your wound. Ask for the reassurance you need in this place. Describe what response you hear and feel.

6. What is the pain and power of your commitment in terms of the nuclear arms race?